Aaree

My First Book **of**
Knowledge

Editor: Katie Puckett
Designer: John Jamieson
Managing Editor: Miranda Smith

Activity illustrations: Gina Suter
Additional design: Joanne Brown
Cover design: Poppy Jenkins
DTP manager: Nicky Studdart
Production controller: Eliot Sedman
Artwork archivists: Wendy Allison, Steve Robinson
Indexer: Rebecca Fairley

KINGFISHER
Kingfisher Publications Plc
New Penderel House
283–288 High Holborn
London WC1V 7HZ
www.kingfisherpub.com

First published by Kingfisher Publications Plc 1999
First published in this format in 2005
10 9 8 7 6 5 4 3 2 1

1TR/0705/TIMS/BESTSET(RAINBOW)/128MA

A CIP catalogue record for this book is available from the British Library.

ISBN-13 978 0 7534 1247 3
ISBN-10 0 7534 1247 0

Printed in China

My First Book of Knowledge

KINGFISHER

Contents

The Universe

The Universe

Everything that exists is part of the Universe. The Earth is in the Universe and so are the Sun, the Moon and everything else in space. The Universe is enormous. No one knows how big it is, or where it begins and ends.

The Universe is made up of billions of stars. Stars are huge balls of burning gases. New stars are born all the time, from clouds of dust and gas. Old stars fade and grow cold.

Some red giants grow into huge supergiants.

A star shines for billions of years.

Then it swells up into a big star called a red giant.

The outer layers of the star may escape into space.

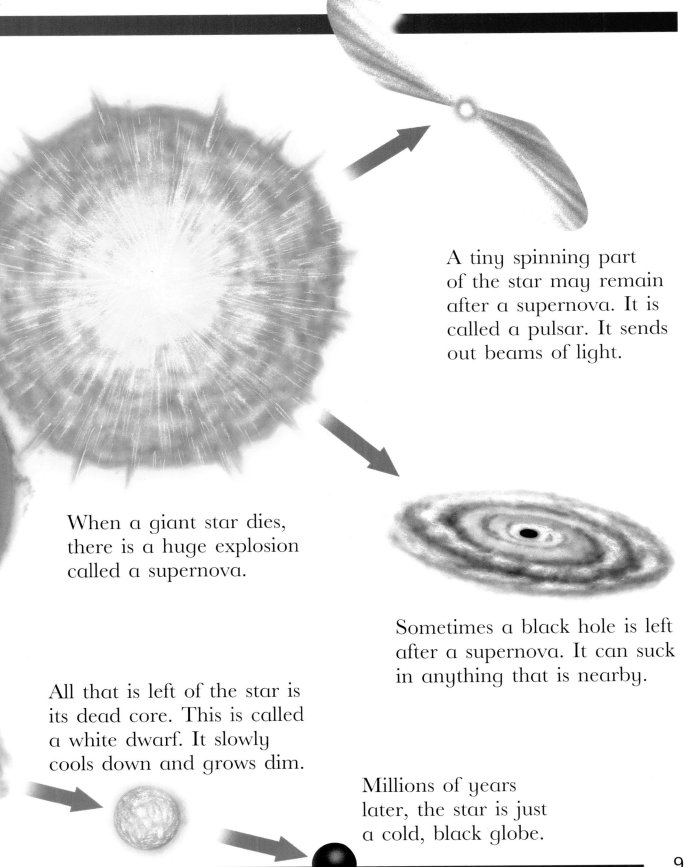

A tiny spinning part of the star may remain after a supernova. It is called a pulsar. It sends out beams of light.

When a giant star dies, there is a huge explosion called a supernova.

Sometimes a black hole is left after a supernova. It can suck in anything that is nearby.

All that is left of the star is its dead core. This is called a white dwarf. It slowly cools down and grows dim.

Millions of years later, the star is just a cold, black globe.

Night sky

On a clear night you can see that the sky is full of stars. Many of them form patterns in the sky, called constellations. Long ago, people gave constellations names to make it easier to recognize them.

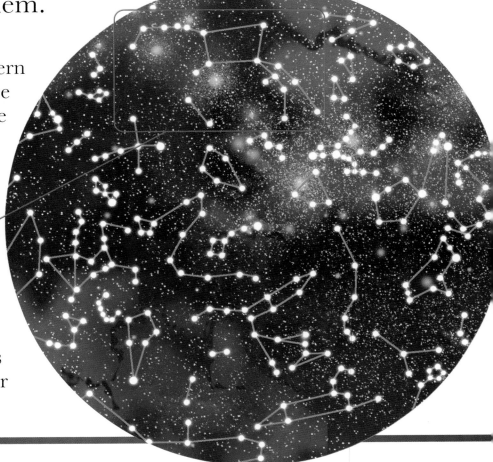

Astronomers use telescopes to look more closely at the stars and to see further into space.

People in the northern part of the world see the stars shown here in the night sky.

This constellation is called Pegasus, after a mythical horse.

10

Space telescopes, such as the Hubble (right), orbit the Earth. They can see much further into space than the largest telescopes on the ground.

People who live in the southern part of the world see a different set of stars. There are more very bright stars here.

This group of stars is known as the Southern Cross.

Galaxies

The Universe is made of gigantic groups of stars called galaxies. There are billions of stars in each galaxy. Planet Earth and the Sun are near the edge of a galaxy called the Milky Way.

If you look at the sky on a clear night, you may see a faint band of stars. This is part of the Milky Way. Our galaxy is a giant spiral of stars, slowly turning around a large group of stars in the middle.

The central part of a galaxy is called the nucleus.

12

New stars form from areas of gas and dust.

Galaxies are different shapes and sizes. These are the three main types.

Irregular-shaped galaxy

Egg-shaped galaxy

Spiral galaxy

The Solar System

A family of planets, moons, comets and other chunks of rock is constantly spinning around the Sun. This family is called the Solar System. There are nine planets in our Solar System. They are made of rocks, liquids, metal or gas.

The planets in the Solar System are millions of kilometres apart. They are very different from one another. Mercury is the closest planet to the Sun, and Pluto is the furthest away. Jupiter is the largest planet. It is so big that all the other planets could fit inside it.

Jupiter

Mercury

Venus

Earth

Mars

14

Orbit

The Sun, the planets and their moons all spin like tops. The planets also travel around the Sun in huge circles. The circular paths they follow are called orbits.

PLANETARIUM

Draw the Sun and planets on card. Colour and cut them out. Attach a piece of thread to each one and hang them from the ceiling in the right order of their distance from the Sun.

Saturn

Uranus

Neptune

Pluto

15

The Sun

Avnee

The Sun is a star, just like the other stars you see in the sky at night. It is an enormous ball of burning gases, millions of times bigger than the Earth. The Sun sends out heat and light. Without it, the Earth would be cold, dark and lifeless.

The Sun's rays can damage your skin if you spend too long outside on a sunny day. People use special cream to protect their skin.

Sun

Earth

The Earth is the third planet from the Sun. It travels around it at a distance of about 150 million kilometres. The Earth moves very fast, but it still takes a year (365 days) to complete its orbit.

The Sun is mostly made of a gas called hydrogen. The hottest part of the Sun is its core. Hot gases bubble up to the surface. They form a halo of gases called the corona. The dark patches on the surface of the Sun are sunspots. They are cooler than the rest of its surface.

Flaming jets of gas can flare up from the surface of the Sun.

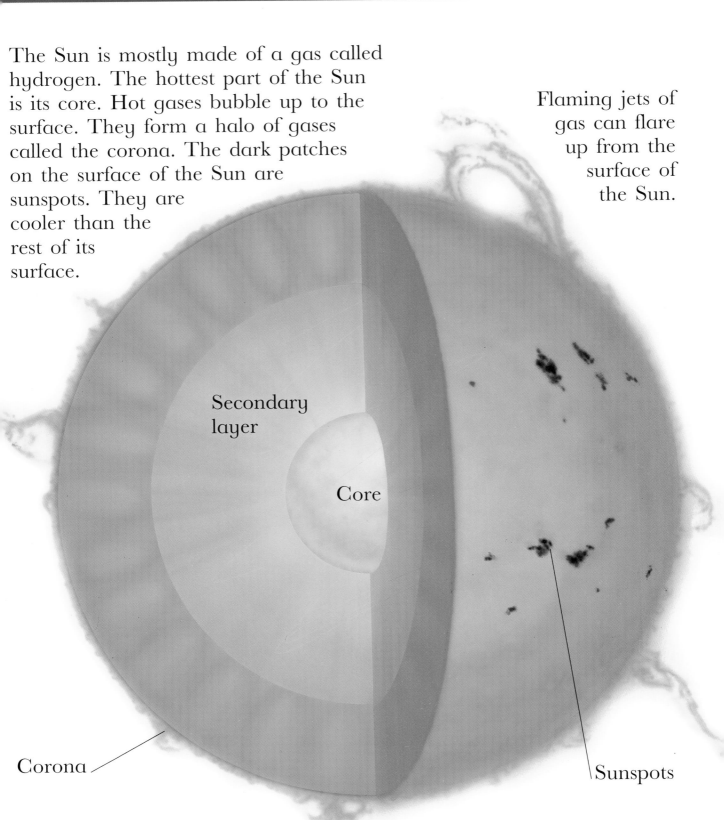

Secondary layer

Core

Corona

Sunspots

Close to the Sun

Mercury and Venus are the two planets in the Solar System that are closest to the Sun. They are both much, much hotter than the Earth. There are no signs of water on either planet. Nothing can grow or live on them.

Mercury spins very slowly, but it races around the Sun. It is burning hot on the side facing the Sun and icy cold on the opposite, dark side.

Mercury is bare and rocky. On the surface it looks a lot like our Moon. It is covered with hills and giant dents called craters.

Venus is about the same size as the Earth. It is the hottest planet of all. Its surface is covered by thick clouds of poisonous gases. These trap heat from the Sun.

You can often see Venus shining brightly in the sky just after sunset or before sunrise. It always looks as if it is quite close to the Sun.

The surface of Venus is mainly flat, but there are lots of old volcanoes, and areas where lava has flowed from the volcanoes. Scientists think some of the volcanoes may still erupt from time to time.

The Earth

The Earth is the planet on which we live. It is a huge ball of rock spinning in space. The Earth is the only planet with water on it, and air for plants and animals to breathe. This is why there is life on Earth, but not on any other planet.

This is what the Earth looks like from out in space. Most of it is covered in blue sea. The brown and green areas are land. The white patterns are clouds swirling in the sky.

The Earth takes a day (24 hours) to spin round once. It is day on the side of the Earth facing the Sun. It is night on whichever side is facing away.

20

Sea

Clouds

Land

NIGHT AND DAY

Hold a globe and ask a friend to shine a torch at it. Then turn the globe. The torch is like the Sun. It is day in the area lit by the torch and night everywhere else.

Spring

Autumn

Summer

Winter

The Earth spins at an angle, so the seasons change as the Earth moves round the Sun. It is summer in the part of the world that is closest to the Sun.

The Moon

The Moon is the closest thing to us in space. It is a little over a quarter the size of the Earth, and takes about a month to travel around it. The Moon has no air, so nothing can grow on it or live there.

The Moon turns as it orbits the Earth, so that the same side of it is always facing the Earth. The dark areas on the Moon are plains.

The surface of the Moon is rocky and dusty. There are thousands of craters. These were made millions of years ago when large rocks from space crashed into the Moon.

| New moon | Half moon, first quarter | Full moon | Half moon, last quarter | Crescent waning |

The Moon seems to change shape. This is because we only see the part of it that is lit by the Sun. The sunlit part changes as the Moon moves around the Earth. Every month the Moon waxes (seems to grow bigger), then wanes (grows smaller).

MOON DIARY

Make a chart with a square for each day of the month. Draw and describe what the Moon looks like every night for a month.

Mars

Mars is the fourth planet from the Sun. It is the planet most like the Earth, but it is much colder because it is further from the Sun. A day on Mars is about the same length as a day on Earth. Mars also has summer and winter seasons.

Mars is often called 'the red planet' because its rocks are a rusty red colour. Winds and storms blow reddish dust about, making Mars look pink from Earth.

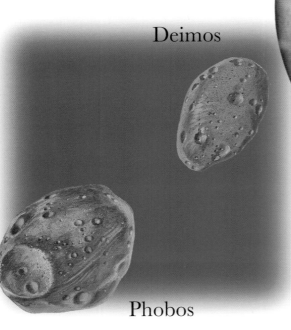

Deimos

Phobos

Mars is circled by two tiny, dark moons, called Phobos and Deimos. They are strangely shaped, rather like lumpy potatoes.

In between Mars and Jupiter, millions of tiny lumps of rock circle the Sun. These mini-planets are called asteroids. Most of them only measure a few kilometres across.

Fragments of rock

Larger rock

Mars is covered with old volcanoes and rocky canyons. Scientists think that there may have been rivers on Mars in the past.

The giant planets

Beyond the asteroids are two enormous gas planets, Jupiter and Saturn. Both of them are circled by rings and moons. Jupiter is the largest planet in the Solar System, larger than all the others put together.

Icy cold clouds cover the surface of Jupiter. Strong winds blow these into bands of different colours.

Swirling clouds

Jupiter has 63 moons. One of them, called Io, has active volcanoes on it. Io's rocky surface (left) is dyed red and orange by sulphur from its volcanoes.

Saturn is a spinning ball of gas and liquid. It is circled by at least 34 rocky moons. The planet's surface is covered in fast-moving clouds.

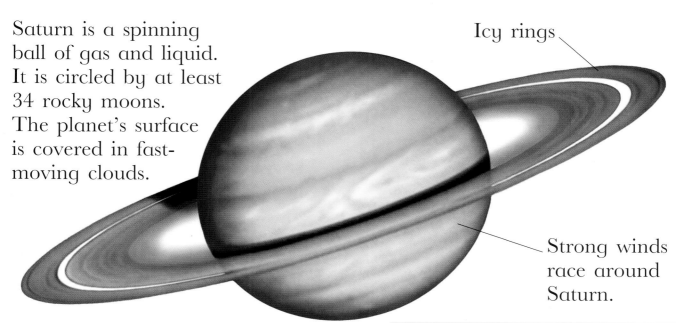

Icy rings

Strong winds race around Saturn.

Saturn's rings are really thousands of narrow ringlets. They are made of millions of bits of glittering ice. Most of these are tiny, but some measure several kilometres across.

MAKE JUPITER

Mix turpentine with drops of red and yellow oil paint. Put drops of colour in a tray of water and swirl them about with a paintbrush. Lay a circle of paper on top. Lift it off and hang it up to dry.

Distant planets

Out near the edge of the Solar System there are three planets; Uranus, Neptune and Pluto. They are so far away that they can't be seen with the naked eye. No space probe has visited Pluto, the most distant planet, so we do not know much about it.

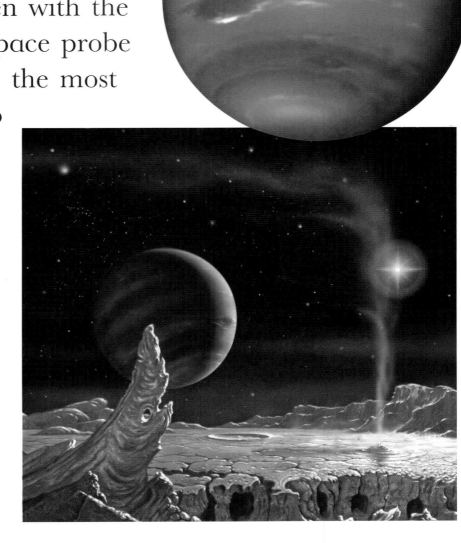

Neptune is a blueish colour. It has 13 moons. Its largest moon, Triton, is the coldest object in the Solar System. Its cracked, frozen surface is dotted with volcanoes. These erupt with plumes of black dust and gases.

Pluto is the smallest
planet of all. It has
one moon, called
Charon, which is
half its size. Pluto
follows an oval-shaped
orbit around the Sun.
This means that it
is sometimes closer to
the Sun than Neptune.

Uranus is four times bigger
than the Earth. It is circled
by 27 moons and about 11
narrow rings of small rocks.

Moving stars

You can see many things in the sky that are not stars or planets. Meteors and comets are burning lumps of rock that look like streaks of light whizzing across the sky.

Meteors are often called shooting stars. Really, they are flecks of space dust which burn up in the air surrounding the Earth.

Lumps of space rock that crash into Earth are called meteorites. Some huge ones like this (right) make massive craters (left).

A comet hangs in the sky like a huge star with a tail. Comets are lumps of ice and rock that orbit the Sun. Their tails can be many millions of kilometres long.

Crumbling pieces of rock and ice

Nucleus

Jets of dust and gas

The Sun's heat melts the surface of the comet, making a cloud of gas and dust that blows into a giant tail.

The World Around Us

About our world

The Earth is amazingly varied. It has hot deserts, huge oceans, steamy rainforests and frozen lands. Each part of the Earth has its own climate, or type of weather. Plants and animals adapt to where they live.

The landscape changes wherever you go. There are natural features, such as mountains. Landmarks such as oil wells have been made by people.

4

6

5

1

3

2

Most of our planet is covered by sea. There is a thin blanket of air surrounding the Earth. This gives us weather.

1. Sea
2. River
3. Lake
4. Rain
5. Waterfall
6. Mountain
7. Forest
8. Oil well
9. Animals
10. City

Volcano

A volcano is a mountain that explodes. Deep beneath the surface of the Earth, the rocks are so hot that they melt. When a volcano erupts, this red-hot melted rock bursts out of a hole at the top of the mountain.

This dog was buried in the lava from a volcano in Pompeii, Italy, in CE79.

ERUPTION!

Make a cone of thick card, leaving a hole at the top. Put a shallow plastic pot in the hole. Add a little red powder paint and some bicarbonate of soda. Carefully add vinegar and watch the volcano erupt.

Lava

Magma

Hot, melted rock is called magma when it is under the ground, and lava when it reaches the surface.

During an eruption, boiling lava pours down the mountain sides, destroying anything in its path. The lava slowly cools in the air. Later it hardens into new rock.

Earthquakes

The top layer of the Earth, its crust, is like a giant jigsaw. It is made of huge interlocking pieces that move about very slowly all the time. Sometimes they do not move smoothly and this makes the ground shake. This is called an earthquake.

An earthquake is very frightening. The ground trembles and buildings may collapse, killing people. Earthquakes usually only last for a few minutes but they cause a lot of damage.

An earthquake happens when two of the Earth's plates, or pieces of its crust, try to move past each other and scrape together. They push and grind in opposite directions, making the rocks tilt and slip.

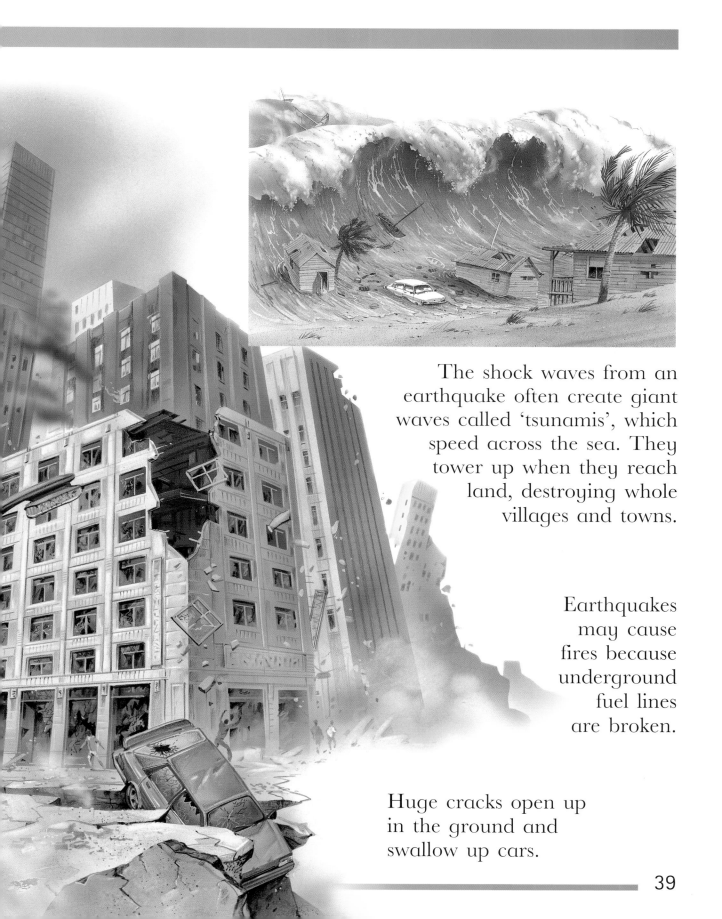

The shock waves from an earthquake often create giant waves called 'tsunamis', which speed across the sea. They tower up when they reach land, destroying whole villages and towns.

Earthquakes may cause fires because underground fuel lines are broken.

Huge cracks open up in the ground and swallow up cars.

Water cycle

The air is full of tiny drops of water too small to see, called water vapour. Rain does not just come from the sky, but from the water that is all around us. The amount of water on Earth stays the same, but it keeps moving around.

The clouds grow heavier and are blown over the land.

Water vapour rises and forms clouds.

Water from the sea turns to water vapour.

As water is warmed by the Sun, it seems to dry up. In fact, it has risen into the air as water vapour. As water vapour rises, it cools down and turns back into drops of water. These form clouds and it rains.

If it is cold, there may be snow instead of rain. The drops of water in the clouds freeze into ice crystals and these join together to make delicate snowflakes. No two snowflakes are ever the same.

Water in the clouds falls as rain, hail, sleet or snow.

Rainwater runs into rivers and flows back into the sea.

MAKE A SNOW STORM

Find a jar with a tight screw-top. Glue cake decorations inside the lid. Pour water into the jar until it is nearly full. Add some glitter and screw on the lid. Shake the jar and turn it upside down.

Life of a river

Many rivers start life in the mountains. Streams of rainwater run from high to low land. They join together and grow into a river. This flows downhill towards the sea.

A river provides food for all kinds of creatures. There are many fish, such as this salmon.

Rain falls high in the mountains.

Streams run into each other.

Waterfall

A river changes with each stage of its journey. It starts life as a bubbling stream, but by the time it reaches the sea it is wider and flows much more slowly.

The river grows wider.

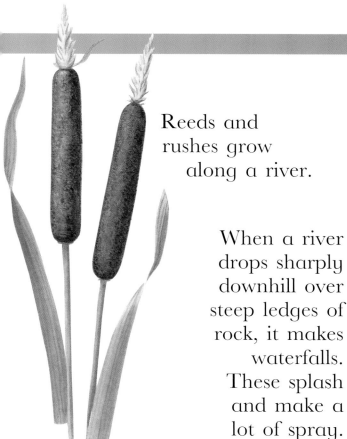

Reeds and rushes grow along a river.

When a river drops sharply downhill over steep ledges of rock, it makes waterfalls. These splash and make a lot of spray.

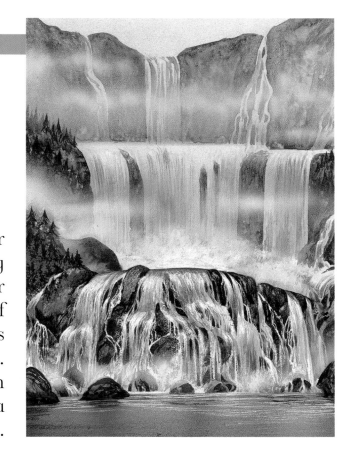

The river winds its way across the land.

All rivers end at the sea. The place where a river flows out into the sea is called the river's mouth.

Saving our planet

There are many problems facing our planet. The air and seas are becoming dirty, or polluted. Plants and animals are dying out. The Earth's natural fuels, such as gas, coal and oil, are being used up.

Fumes from factories and cars pollute the air with chemicals. These dissolve in clouds and make acid rain, which falls to the ground and harms wildlife and plants.

Factory fumes

Acid rain

Chemicals draining into the river

Traffic fumes

Scientists are inventing new forms of energy that do not cause pollution. They can use energy from the Sun or wind to make electricity.

Solar-powered electric car

RECYCLE IT!

Sort your family's rubbish into boxes for paper, glass and aluminium cans. Take them to your local recycling centre.

Animals are hunted and their homes are destroyed or polluted. The humpback whale (below) has been hunted so much that it may die out.

Humpback whale

Prehistoric Life

Evolution

The Earth is millions of years old and is slowly changing all the time. As the Earth changes, so do the plants and animals that live here. They adapt to suit where they live. The way that living things change is called evolution.

The first tiny fish lived in the sea about 500 million years ago.

About 395 million years ago some animals moved on to the land. These were the amphibians.

Nearly all of the animals that live on Earth today did not exist in the past. Most of the animals that lived in the past no longer exist today. The first plants and animals were tiny and lived in the sea. Nowadays there are all sorts of living things on every part of the planet.

Some animals die out, or become extinct, if their homes and lives are disturbed. The dodo was a large flightless bird that lived on the island of Mauritius. It was hunted by the people who first settled on the island and is now extinct.

Dinosaurs and other reptiles lived from 240 million years ago to 64 million years ago.

After the dinosaurs died out, there were more mammals. The first ones were small, but later ones were bigger.

The first humans lived about two million years ago. They may have evolved from ape-like creatures.

Dinosaur world

Dinosaurs appeared on our planet 228 million years ago. Some of them were enormous. They were the biggest animals ever to live on land. Others were not much bigger than a chicken. All of them died out 64 million years ago.

All dinosaurs had scaly skins and laid eggs, like reptiles do today. Some ate plants, while others were hunters. They lived alongside other reptiles and early kinds of birds and insects.

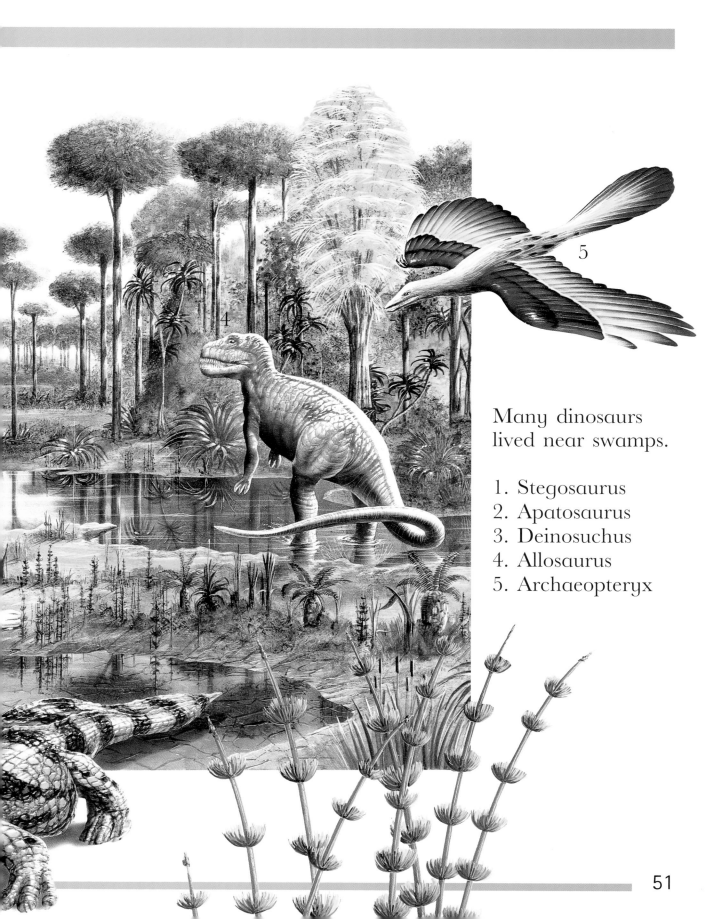

Many dinosaurs
lived near swamps.

1. Stegosaurus
2. Apatosaurus
3. Deinosuchus
4. Allosaurus
5. Archaeopteryx

Plant-eaters

The biggest dinosaurs of all were plant-eaters. They had barrel-shaped bodies and very long necks and tails. These giants lived in herds and moved from place to place looking for food. They plucked leaves from high in trees, like giraffes do today.

The weather was warm and wet at the time of the dinosaurs. There were forests of giant ferns and evergreens. Plant-eaters ate leaves, roots and pine cones. They had peg-like teeth for snipping leaves off trees.

1. Brachiosaurus
2. Apatosaurus
3. Diplodocus

Some plant-eaters looked very strange. One was called Parasaurolophus. These dinosaurs had mouths like beaks and bony crests on their heads. They could blow out through these, and may have tooted like trombones.

2

3

DINOSAUR INVITE

Draw and colour a long-necked dinosaur on a wide piece of card. Write your party instructions on the back. Make it into a concertina shape by folding the card as shown.

Meat-eaters

Some dinosaurs ate animals and other dinosaurs. Most meat-eaters were very fierce and could move fast to catch their prey. Some of them hunted alone. Others hunted in packs.

Tyrannosaurus Rex was the biggest meat-eater of all. It had massive jaws and razor-sharp teeth for slicing through flesh.

Many meat-eaters had huge hooked claws for slashing out at the animals they chased.

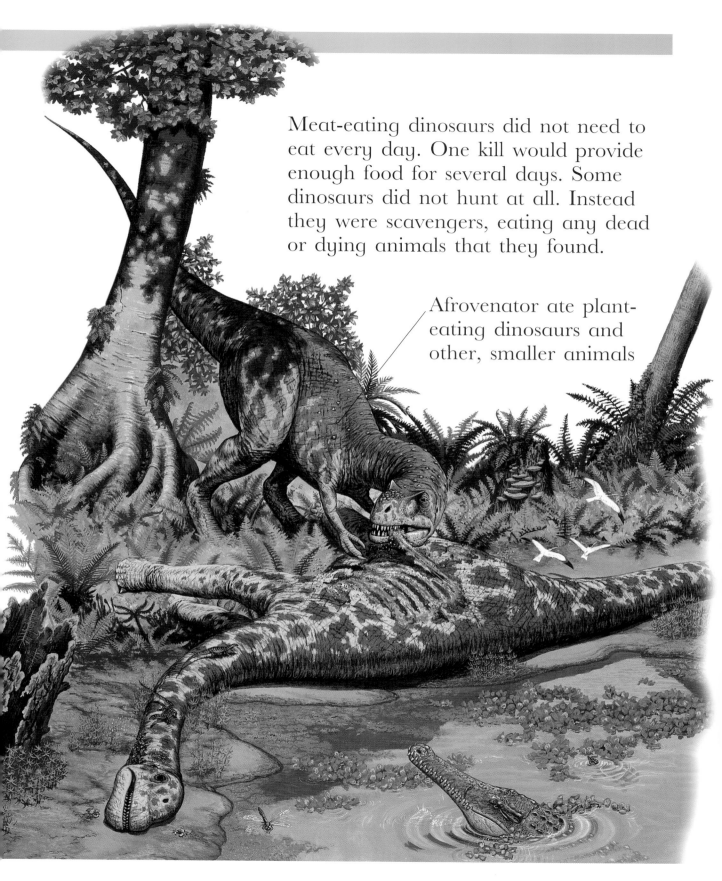

Meat-eating dinosaurs did not need to eat every day. One kill would provide enough food for several days. Some dinosaurs did not hunt at all. Instead they were scavengers, eating any dead or dying animals that they found.

Afrovenator ate plant-eating dinosaurs and other, smaller animals

Into battle

Plant-eating dinosaurs could not move fast, so they had to be able to defend themselves against hungry meat-eaters. Some plant-eaters grouped together for safety. Others had fierce horns to scare off enemies, and thick skin like armour.

Deinonychus was a small, fast meat-eater. Its name means 'terrible claw' because it had long, curved claws on its back feet. Deinonychus was too small to kill a large plant-eater on its own, so it hunted in a pack. The pack would attack together, wounding their victim with their claws and teeth.

Triceratops was armed with horns on its nose and above its eyes. It also had a huge bony neck shield and thick, leathery skin to protect it from enemies.

This armoured dinosaur was called Euoplocephalus. It had bony plates and spikes along its back and a huge club at the end of its tail.

A TRICERATOPS MASK

Draw a Triceratops face like this on thick card. Make a nose horn out of card and attach it to the mask with a paper fastener.

Tie a thin piece of elastic through holes at the sides of the mask.

Hatching out

Avnee ✓

Dinosaur babies hatched from eggs, just as reptiles do today. Some dinosaur mothers, including Maiasaura, made big nests on the ground in which they laid about 20 eggs. In 1984, a group of more than 20 Maiasaura nests was found on Egg Mountain in the United States.

Dinosaur eggs

Fossils of dinosaur eggs are found in different shapes and sizes.

When a herd of long-necked dinosaurs set off, the little ones walked in the middle, guarded by the enormous grown-ups.

When Maiasaura babies
hatched out, their mother
brought them tender
young plants to eat.
After a few weeks,
the babies could look
for their own food.

This baby dinosaur is
curled up inside its egg.

Nest built
inside
an earth
mound

Giants of the sea

While dinosaurs ruled the land, many fierce reptiles lived in the sea. Some of them were fast swimmers and looked like dolphins. Others were like lizards, or had strange long necks and giant flippers like paddles.

Kronosaurus had a huge head bigger than a car.

Mosasaurus was a fierce sea lizard. It crunched small sea creatures in its powerful jaws.

Elasmosaurus had
a long snake-like neck.
It may have swum along
holding its neck and tiny
head above the water.

Ichthyosaurus looked
like one of today's
dolphins. It was a
fast swimmer and
might have hunted in
shoals. It ate fish and
creatures like squid.

Teleosaurus was a sea crocodile.
It was quick to snap up fish in its long
snout, which was armed with sharp teeth.

Take to the skies

The first creatures to fly were insects, 300 million years ago. Then reptiles called pterosaurs took to the air. They glided through the skies, soaring above the dinosaurs on the land.

Archaeopteryx was the first creature with feathers. It was half-dinosaur and half-bird. No one knows if it could fly.

Quetzalcoatlus was a giant pterosaur, much, much bigger than even the largest birds today. Its huge wings were made of skin, like a bat's wings. It had a furry body and no feathers or teeth.

The first insects with wings were dragonflies. Meganeura was a huge dragonfly with a wingspan of about 75 centimetres.

FLY A PTEROSAUR

Tie two canes together, one twice as long as the other. Ask an adult to cut notches in the ends. Tie a piece of string to each corner to make a frame. Lay the frame on a clear plastic bag. Cut around it, 5 cm outside. Stretch the bag across the frame and tape the edges down. Cut out a pterosaur and tape it to the kite. Tie on some string.

Extinction

Dinosaurs lived on the Earth for 165 million years before they became extinct, dying out for ever. All the flying reptiles, sea reptiles and many other animals died out at the same time. No one knows exactly why.

There are many ideas about why the dinosaurs disappeared. Some people think that mammals might have stolen and eaten too many dinosaur eggs. Others think that the weather and living conditions changed, and that it may have become too hot or too cold for the dinosaurs.

Scientists think that a giant meteorite crashed into the Earth about 65 million years ago. Dust from the crash may have blocked out the Sun, so that it was cold and no plants could grow. Plant-eating animals would have starved to death. Meat-eaters would have soon died out too, when there were no other animals for them to eat.

First people

For most of the Earth's history, there have been no humans. The first people like us lived only about 100,000 years ago. They may have been related to ape-like creatures that lived earlier.

People living 15,000 years ago survived by hunting, fishing and gathering plants to eat. They moved from place to place in search of food, and sheltered in caves or tents.

Some people lived in caves. They painted pictures of the animals they hunted on their cave walls, using colours made from crushed rocks.

Making a fire

People hunted woolly mammoths. They were huge and had long, thick hair to protect them from the cold weather.

A WOOLLY MAMMOTH

Draw a big woolly mammoth on a large piece of thick paper or card, copying the picture on the right. Colour in its tusks, toes and eyes. To make its hairy coat, cut short pieces of reddish-brown wool and glue them to your picture. If you want to, you can cut it out.

Making tools

Early people were good at making things with their hands. Remains found in their caves show that they made knives and weapons from sharp stones and tools from antlers, bones and mammoth tusks.

Plant Life

Plants everywhere

There are millions of different kinds of plants and they grow nearly everywhere in the world. They can be all shapes and sizes, from tiny mosses to enormous trees. Some spring up after rain in hot, dry deserts. Others flower in snowy cracks high on mountains.

In steamy rainforests, many plants grow high above the ground on sunny tree branches. These plants are called epiphytes. They soak up all the water they need from the damp air or collect rainwater in their cup-shaped leaves.

Like many plants, the rose has beautiful flowers. Roses often smell sweet.

Acorn

Oak tree

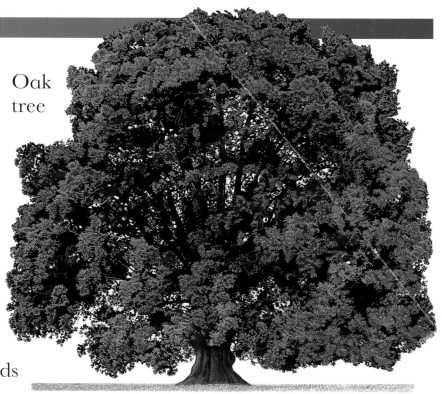

Trees are the largest plants in the world. Some, such as the oak, can live to be hundreds of years old. The oak produces seeds called acorns.

Fungi are not plants. They do not have leaves or roots, and they are not green. Instead of seeds, they produce spores.

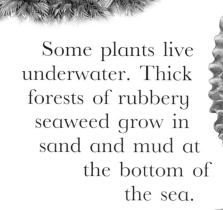

Some plants live underwater. Thick forests of rubbery seaweed grow in sand and mud at the bottom of the sea.

71

Food for growth

Plants need food and water to grow. Their roots take water from the soil and their leaves soak up air and sunlight. Plants use water, air and sunlight to make their own food.

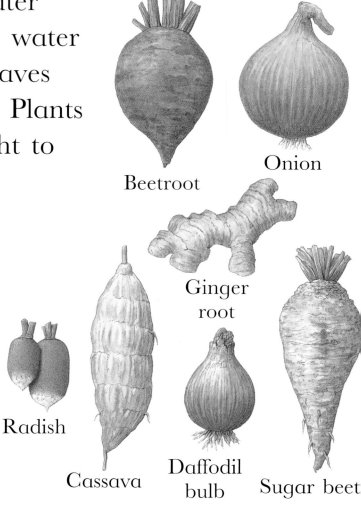

Beetroot

Onion

Ginger root

Radish

Cassava

Daffodil bulb

Sugar beet

TAKE A CUTTING

Spider plants grow baby plants at the ends of runners.
Snip off a baby plant and put it in a glass of water. When it has grown roots, plant it in a small pot of moist compost.

All plants have roots. Some plants have fat roots, others have swollen buds or stems under the ground. These are a kind of food store. Plants use the food stored in them to grow when conditions are right.

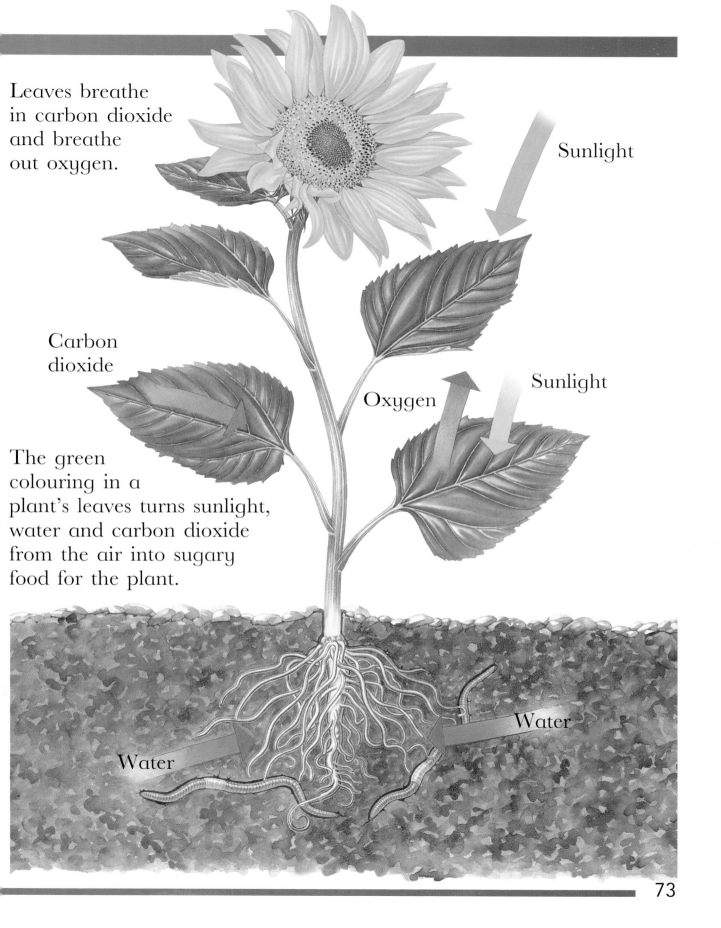

Leaves breathe in carbon dioxide and breathe out oxygen.

Sunlight

Carbon dioxide

Oxygen

Sunlight

The green colouring in a plant's leaves turns sunlight, water and carbon dioxide from the air into sugary food for the plant.

Water

Water

Flowers

There are flowers of nearly every colour, and many different shapes – bells, circles, stars and trumpets. Garden flowers are are often the showy relatives of simple wild flowers.

A meadow is full of flowers in the spring and summer. Butterflies and other insects visit the flowers because they like their colour and scent.

Poppies

Buttercups

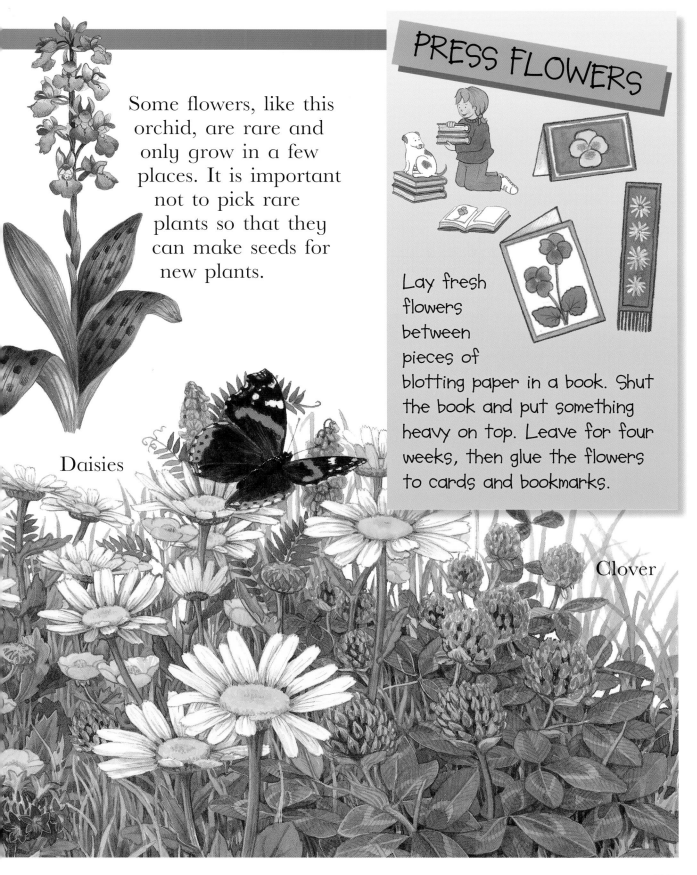

Some flowers, like this orchid, are rare and only grow in a few places. It is important not to pick rare plants so that they can make seeds for new plants.

PRESS FLOWERS

Lay fresh flowers between pieces of blotting paper in a book. Shut the book and put something heavy on top. Leave for four weeks, then glue the flowers to cards and bookmarks.

Daisies

Clover

Making seeds

To make seeds, a flower needs pollen from another flower. Most flowers contain a sweet juice called nectar to attract birds and insects. As they drink, they brush against pollen, which they carry from flower to flower. This is called pollination.

Tiny hummingbirds pollinate some flowers in hot countries. They push their beaks right into the flowers to reach the nectar inside.

Pollen

Hibiscus flowers attract hummingbirds.

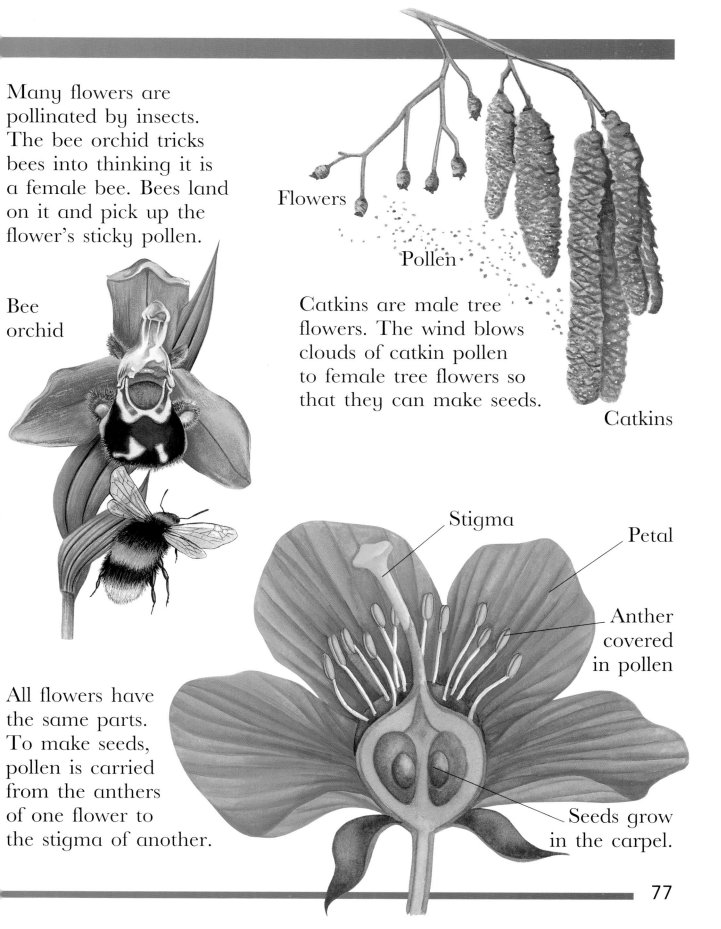

Many flowers are pollinated by insects. The bee orchid tricks bees into thinking it is a female bee. Bees land on it and pick up the flower's sticky pollen.

Bee orchid

Flowers

Pollen

Catkins are male tree flowers. The wind blows clouds of catkin pollen to female tree flowers so that they can make seeds.

Catkins

Stigma

Petal

Anther covered in pollen

All flowers have the same parts. To make seeds, pollen is carried from the anthers of one flower to the stigma of another.

Seeds grow in the carpel.

Fruits and berries

After a flower has been pollinated, seeds start to grow. They are protected by a soft fruit which grows around the seeds. Some fruits only contain one big seed or pip. Berries have lots of tiny seeds inside them.

In the autumn, hedges are full of ripe, juicy berries. These are eaten by birds and animals. Later, the seeds inside the berries are scattered on the ground in bird and animal droppings.

Look for these berries in the picture:

1. Hawthorn berries
2. Rosehips
3. Blackberries
4. Elderberries
5. Rowan berries

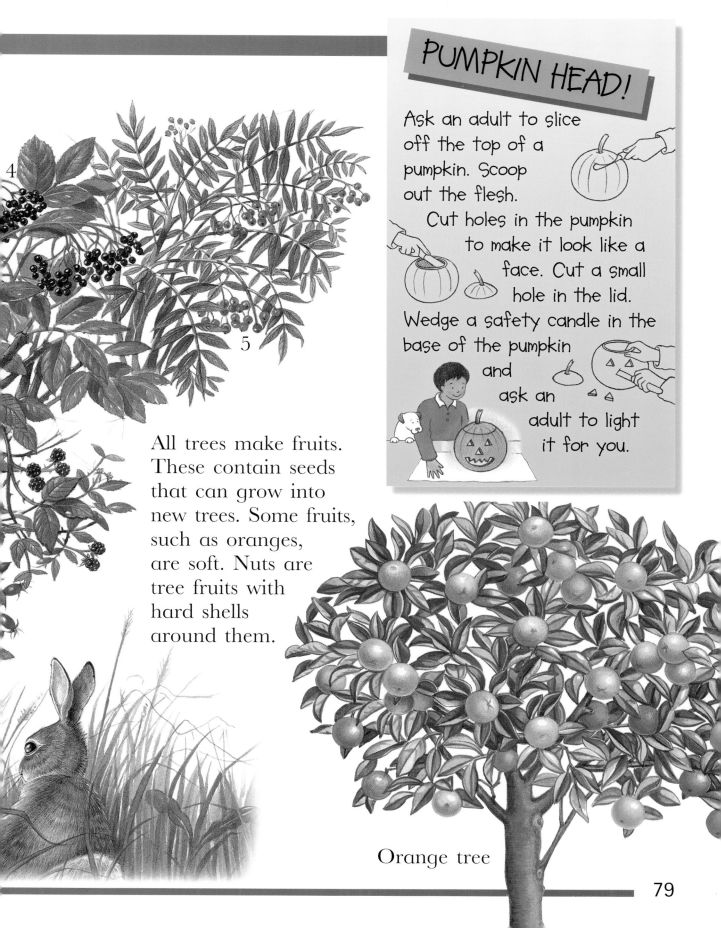

4

5

All trees make fruits. These contain seeds that can grow into new trees. Some fruits, such as oranges, are soft. Nuts are tree fruits with hard shells around them.

PUMPKIN HEAD!

Ask an adult to slice off the top of a pumpkin. Scoop out the flesh.

Cut holes in the pumpkin to make it look like a face. Cut a small hole in the lid.

Wedge a safety candle in the base of the pumpkin and ask an adult to light it for you.

Orange tree

Seeds

Most plants grow from seeds which fall on the ground. In spring, the soil is damp and warm. This makes each seed swell and start to grow. The root grows first, then a shoot. This is called germination.

Seeds inside berries often reach the ground in birds' droppings.

Dandelion seeds are blown to the ground by the wind.

Bean seed

When a seed germinates, it splits open and a root begins to grow. A leafy shoot pushes up through the soil towards the light. Leaves help the plant to make its own food.

Root Shoot

80

First real leaves

Stem

Put some tissue paper in two clean eggshells. Sprinkle cress seeds on top and keep the tissue damp. In ten days you will be able to cut some cress.

Some seeds are hidden inside soft, juicy fruit. Others have hard shells to protect them and are called nuts.

Horse chestnut

Peach

Pine cone

Sycamore

Plants and animals

Without plants, there would not be any animals. Plants provide all kinds of animals with food and homes. In return, animals help to scatter the seeds that will grow into new plants.

Harvest mouse

Harvest mice eat grass seeds, like lots of other small animals. The spiky seedheads of some plants stick to their fur and are carried to different places, where the seeds fall off and grow.

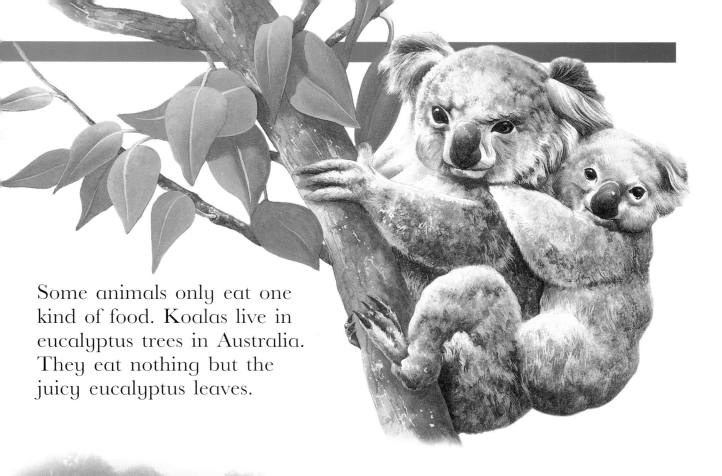

Some animals only eat one kind of food. Koalas live in eucalyptus trees in Australia. They eat nothing but the juicy eucalyptus leaves.

Goldfinches also feed on seeds. They crush them in their beaks. Some of the seeds are scattered on the ground in birds' droppings.

Leaf-cutter ants snip up leaves and carry them to their nest, where they are chewed into a pulp. The ants feed on fungus that grows on the leaves.

Plants we eat

Many of the things we eat and drink are made from plants. Fruits and vegetables come from plants, and so do flour, sugar, coffee and chocolate. Nearly all plant foods are grown as crops by farmers around the world.

The vegetables we eat come from different parts of vegetable plants. Some are roots, such as carrots. Others may come from the leaves, stems, pods or seeds of plants.

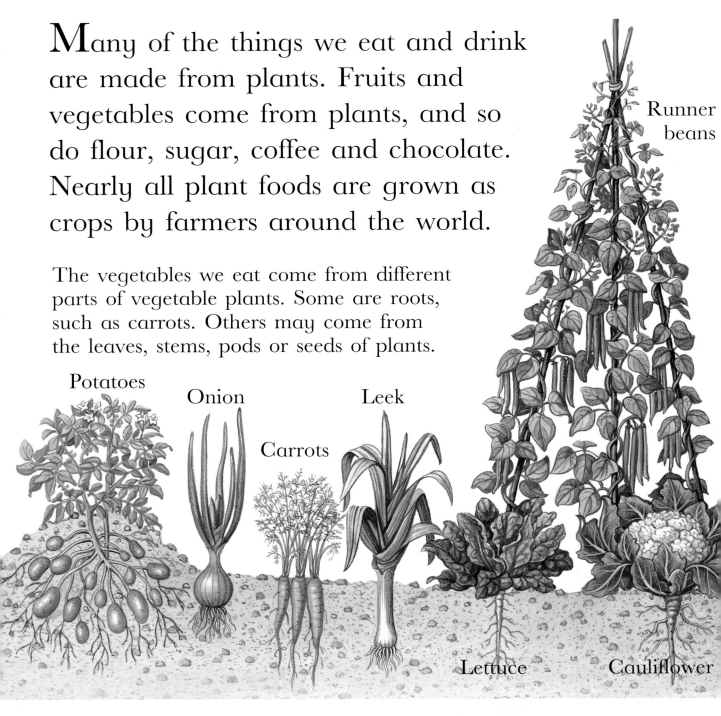

Runner beans

Potatoes

Onion

Carrots

Leek

Lettuce

Cauliflower

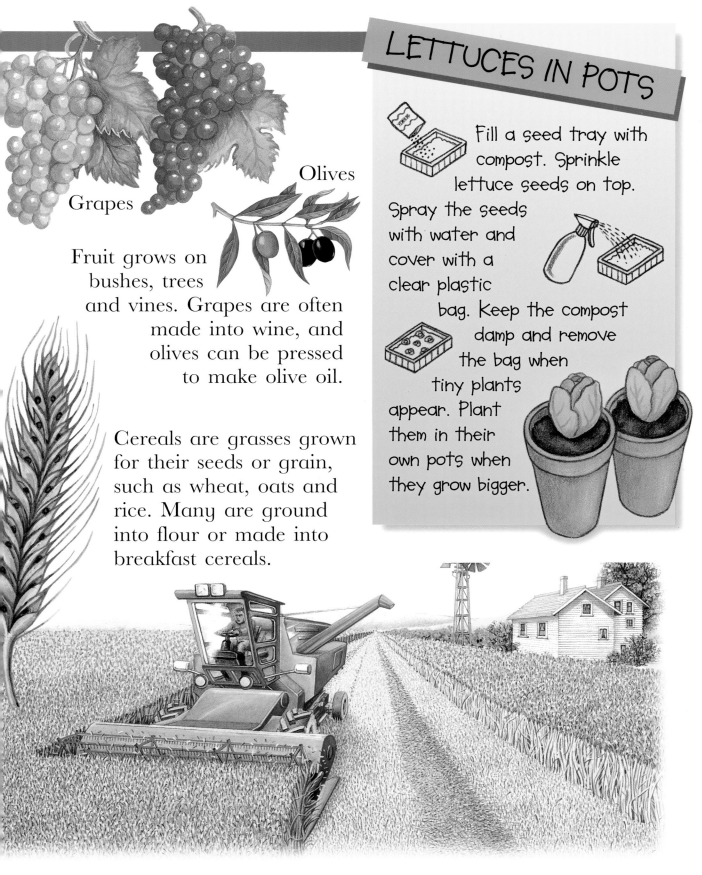

Grapes

Olives

Fruit grows on bushes, trees and vines. Grapes are often made into wine, and olives can be pressed to make olive oil.

Cereals are grasses grown for their seeds or grain, such as wheat, oats and rice. Many are ground into flour or made into breakfast cereals.

LETTUCES IN POTS

Fill a seed tray with compost. Sprinkle lettuce seeds on top. Spray the seeds with water and cover with a clear plastic bag. Keep the compost damp and remove the bag when tiny plants appear. Plant them in their own pots when they grow bigger.

Animal
World

What is a reptile?

Snakes, lizards, crocodiles and turtles are all reptiles. They have dry, scaly skin. Reptiles are cold-blooded. This means that their bodies are the same temperature as their surroundings. They lie in the Sun to warm up, then hide in the shade to cool down.

Most reptiles hatch from eggs, like this baby snake. Reptile eggs do not have hard shells. Instead, they are soft and leathery.

Gecko

Snakes and lizards, such as this gecko, shed their skins as they grow. A new layer of skin is ready underneath.

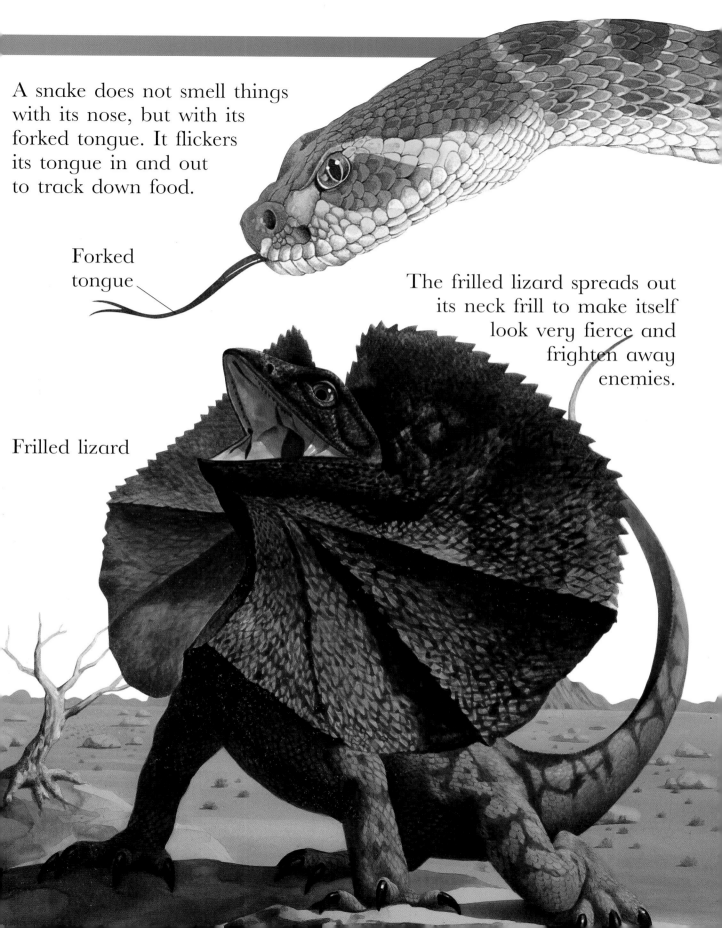

A snake does not smell things with its nose, but with its forked tongue. It flickers its tongue in and out to track down food.

Forked tongue

The frilled lizard spreads out its neck frill to make itself look very fierce and frighten away enemies.

Frilled lizard

Lizards

Geckos, iguanas, skinks and chameleons are all lizards. They usually live on the ground, but some spend their lives scuttling about in the treetops or burrowing under the ground. Most lizards eat insects.

Many lizards are brightly coloured and patterned. This eyed lizard gets its name from the blue spots along its sides.

The Gila monster is a poisonous lizard. It makes poison in its mouth and bites small animals to kill them.

90

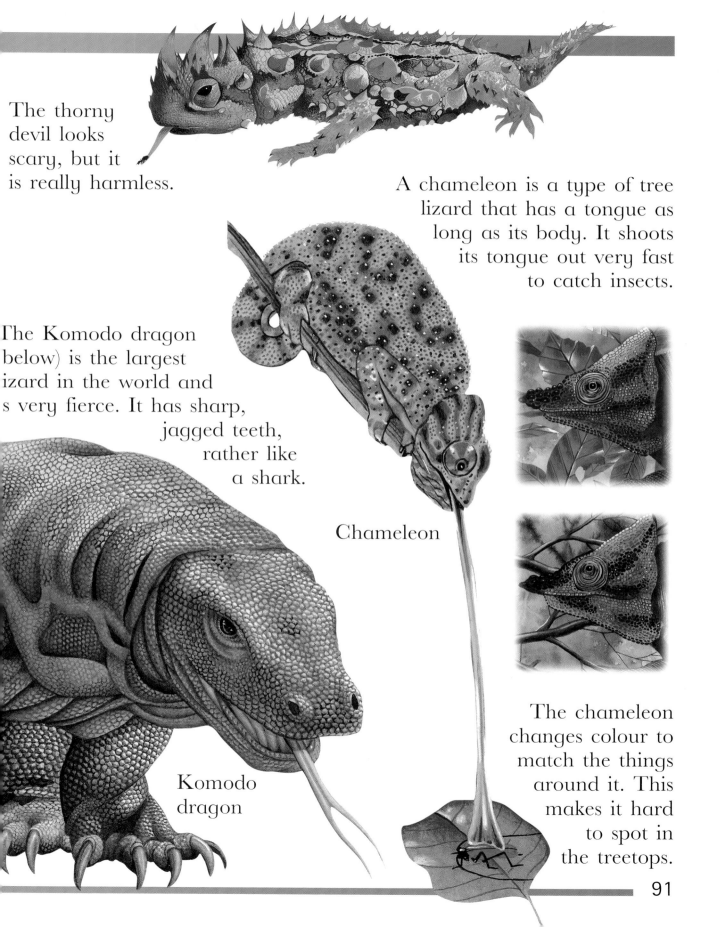

The thorny devil looks scary, but it is really harmless.

A chameleon is a type of tree lizard that has a tongue as long as its body. It shoots its tongue out very fast to catch insects.

The Komodo dragon below) is the largest izard in the world and s very fierce. It has sharp, jagged teeth, rather like a shark.

Chameleon

Komodo dragon

The chameleon changes colour to match the things around it. This makes it hard to spot in the treetops.

Turtles

Turtles and tortoises are the only reptiles with a heavy shell to protect them from enemies. Tortoises usually live on land. Turtles live in the sea and can swim quickly with their strong flippers. Turtles and tortoises both lay their eggs on land.

2. The turtle digs a hole. She lays her eggs in it and covers them with sand.

1. A turtle swims to a sandy beach at night to lay her eggs.

3. When the baby turtles hatch, they climb out of the sand and run to the sea.

A tortoise moves very slowly. When something scares it, it tucks its head and legs right inside its shell.

Make a hole in each side of a paper bowl. Thread elastic through the holes and tie the ends. Glue brown paper patches round the bottom of the bowl. Glue card eyes to the middle finger of a glove. Put on the glove and wear the bowl on top.

Giant tortoises live on the Galapagos Islands. They may live for up to 50 years and grow to be one metre long.

Crocodiles

Crocodiles usually live in rivers in hot countries. They spend most of their time lying in the water, waiting for animals to come to drink. Then they lunge forward to attack. Few animals can escape their sharp teeth.

Crocodiles float with their eyes and nose above the surface.

Alligator

Garial

Caiman

The three animals above are all related to the crocodile. Each one has a different snout.

An alligator (above) lies on a sunny riverbank to warm up. It cools down by wallowing in deep pools of water.

A mother crocodile (below) looks after her eggs. When they hatch, she carries the babies gently down to the river in her huge mouth.

Frogs

Frogs live in many different places. Some can even be found high up in the treetops. All frogs lay their eggs in water. The tiny creatures that hatch do not look like frogs at first, but they change as they grow. This is called metamorphosis.

A frog can leap a long way because its back legs are like springs. It starts with them folded. To jump, it unfolds its long back legs and springs forwards.

1. A frog lays hundreds of eggs. The eggs are laid in clear jelly. They are called frogspawn.

2. Tadpoles grow inside the eggs.

Mother frog

Tree frogs have sticky pads on their fingers and toes to help them grip on to branches.

3. The eggs hatch into tadpoles.

4. The tadpoles grow bigger and develop legs.

5. The tadpoles turn into frogs and leave the water.

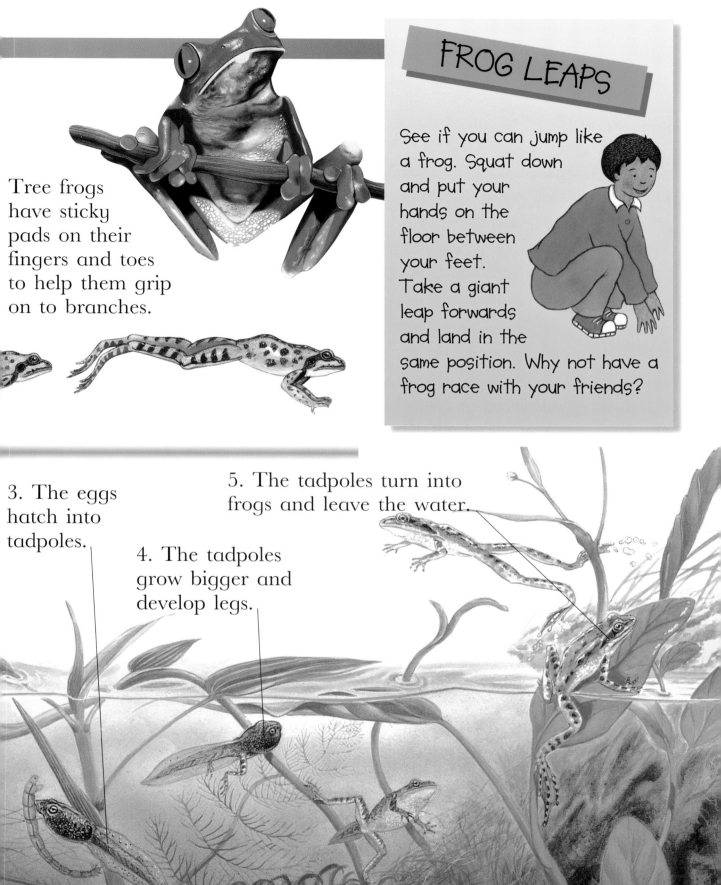

What is a fish?

Fish live in water and are amazing swimmers. Some fish are as small as tadpoles and others longer than crocodiles. Some are flat and others tube-shaped. But most fish have the same basic features.

Slippery scales on a fish's body help it to glide smoothly through the water.

Most fish lay eggs. They lay hundreds of tiny eggs at a time.

Fish use their fins to steer and turn as they swim.

A fish does not have any eyelids, so it always swims with its eyes wide open.

Some fish live in the sea, where the water is salty. Others live in rivers and lakes. These are called freshwater fish.

Fish have slits called gills on the sides of their heads so that they can breathe underwater.

A fish swims along by beating its tail from side to side.

AN AQUARIUM

Paint the inside of a box blue-green. Turn the box on its side and put pebbles and shells inside it. Draw, colour and cut out pretty fish. Tape a string to each fish and tape them to the top of the box.

Coral fish

Thousands of brightly coloured fish dart through the clear blue waters around a coral reef. Corals grow in many shapes and colours, like a rocky garden under the sea. The water is shallow and sunny, and there is plenty to eat.

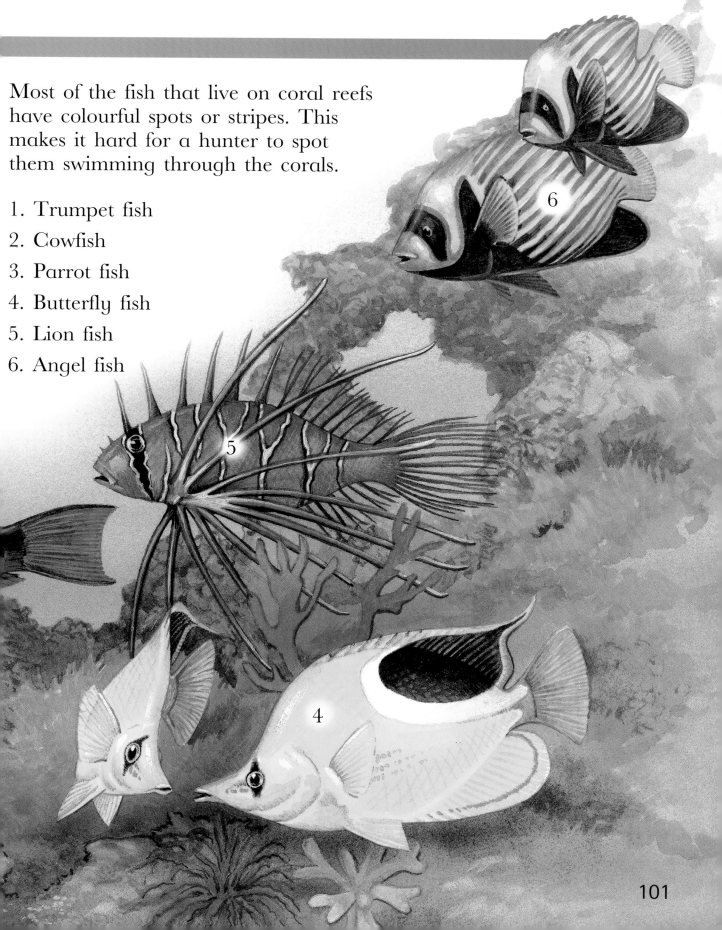

Most of the fish that live on coral reefs have colourful spots or stripes. This makes it hard for a hunter to spot them swimming through the corals.

1. Trumpet fish
2. Cowfish
3. Parrot fish
4. Butterfly fish
5. Lion fish
6. Angel fish

Sea hunters

Many of the creatures that live in the sea feed on plants, but others are fierce and deadly hunters. Some sea hunters rely on speed to catch their prey, but others have more unusual ways of finding their food.

The great white shark hunts by scent. When the shark smells food, it charges towards it with amazing speed. The shark snaps its prey up in its huge jaws and swallows it whole.

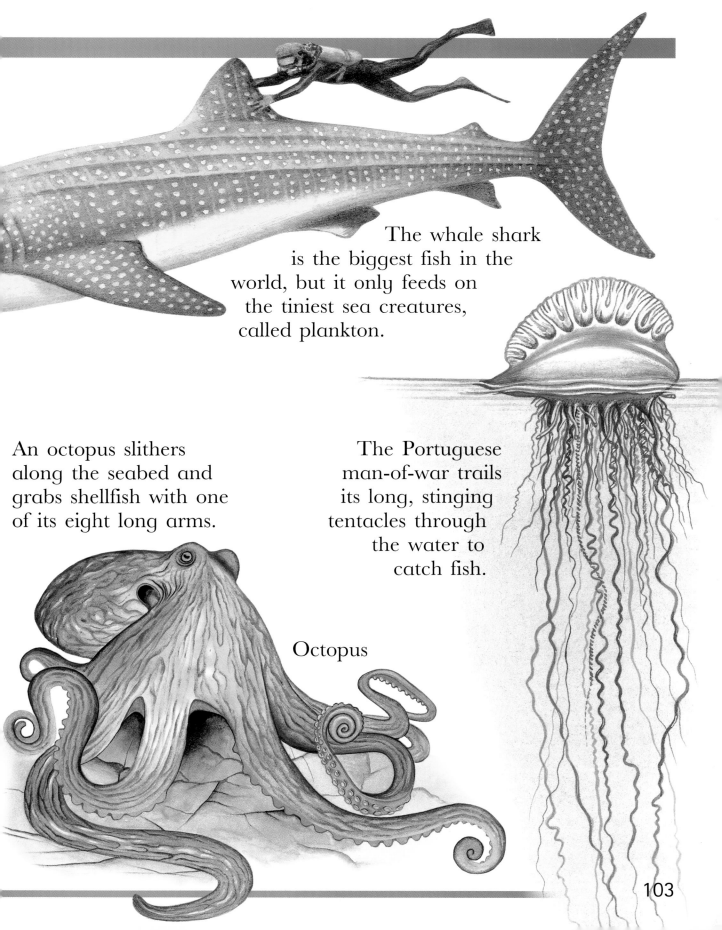

The whale shark
is the biggest fish in the
world, but it only feeds on
the tiniest sea creatures,
called plankton.

An octopus slithers
along the seabed and
grabs shellfish with one
of its eight long arms.

The Portuguese
man-of-war trails
its long, stinging
tentacles through
the water to
catch fish.

Octopus

What is an insect?

Most insects are small. Their bodies are made up of three parts – a head, a thorax (middle), and an abdomen (back part). An insect has six legs and two antennae. Its body is protected by a hard outer case.

Thorax

Head

Antennae

Proboscis

The wings of the brightly coloured shield bug are hidden beneath the large stripy shield on its back.

Honey bees feed on nectar, a sweet juice inside flowers. They suck up the nectar through a feeding tube called a proboscis. Honey bees also collect flower pollen.

 Ants live in colonies.

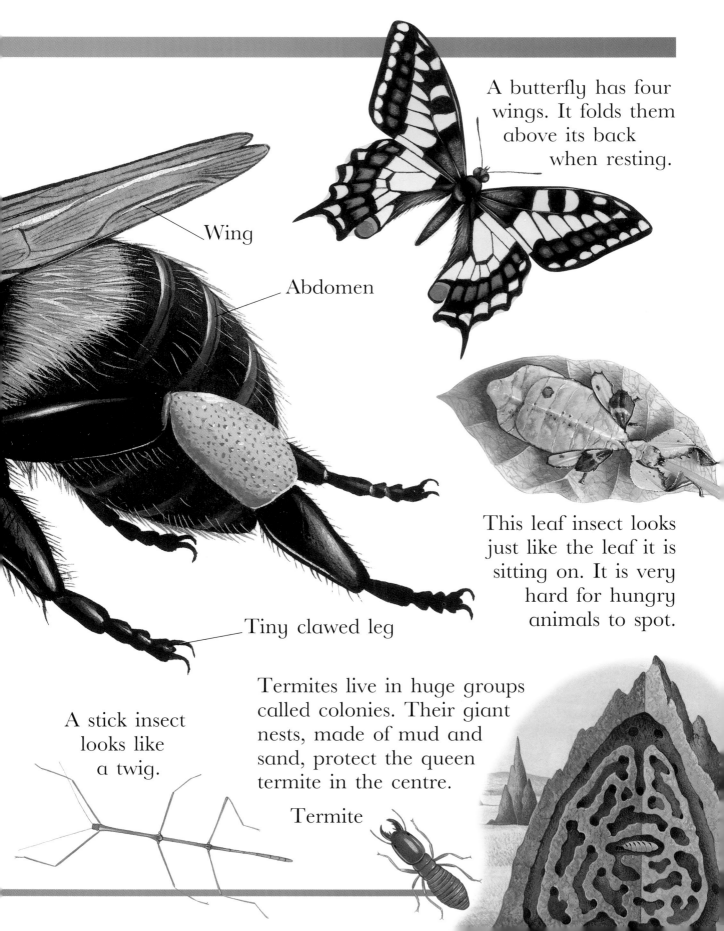

Wing

Abdomen

Tiny clawed leg

A butterfly has four wings. It folds them above its back when resting.

This leaf insect looks just like the leaf it is sitting on. It is very hard for hungry animals to spot.

A stick insect looks like a twig.

Termites live in huge groups called colonies. Their giant nests, made of mud and sand, protect the queen termite in the centre.

Termite

Butterflies

On a warm summer's day, butterflies flutter from flower to flower, feeding on nectar. The beautiful patterns on a butterfly's wings are made of thousands of brightly coloured overlapping scales. Moths are like butterflies, but fly at night.

Monarch butterfly

A butterfly begins life as a wriggly caterpillar. It has to change completely before it becomes a butterfly.

1. A butterfly lays its eggs on a plant.

2. The eggs hatch into caterpillars.

3. The caterpillars eat and grow bigger.

Tiger moth

Moths have fatter bodies than butterflies and their antennae are not as thick as butterfly antennae. Moth antennae are feathery or look like hairs.

The death's head moth has a shape like a skull on the back of its head.

Cinnabar moth

4. Each caterpillar turns into a pupa.

5. A butterfly breaks out of the pupa.

Minibeasts

There are many tiny creatures that are not insects and cannot fly. Most of them hide away among plants or stones during the day. They usually come out to look for food at night, or just after it has rained.

An earthworm eats the soil as it wriggles its way through. It has no eyes, ears or legs.

Sting

Scorpions usually live in hot countries. They are very fierce. A scorpion catches prey in its giant pincers and kills it with the poisonous sting at the end of its tail.

Pincer

The hairy tarantula is one of the biggest spiders in the world.

A centipede has lots of tiny legs. There is one pair of legs on each segment of its body.

HAIRY SPIDER

Make a pompom by winding wool around two card discs with holes in. Push four pipe cleaners through the holes. Cut round the edge of the card and tie some wool round the middle. Take out the card. Bend the pipe cleaners to make legs, and stick on eyes.

Snails slither along the ground, leaving trails of slime behind them. If they are scared, they quickly draw back into their shells.

What is a bird?

There are thousands of different birds of every colour, shape and size. Birds are the only animals that have feathers, and most birds can fly. The smallest bird is no bigger than a butterfly. The largest is taller than a man.

The tiny wren is only about as long as your finger.

A bird's body is a clever flying machine. Birds have very light bones and strong wing muscles to make it easier to fly. Their feathers keep them warm and dry. A bird's tail helps it to steer and brake when it is flying.

The shape of a bird's beak shows what kind of food it eats. The toucan's giant bill is good for plucking fruit.

The ostrich cannot fly. It is the biggest and heaviest bird of all.

The peregrine's smooth shape helps it to fly and dive very fast.

Birds of prey

Birds of prey are fierce hunters with sharp beaks and claws, and very good eyesight. They soar high in the sky, hunting for small animals or fish. When they spot an animal moving beneath them, they drop down from the sky and kill it.

Eagles are the biggest birds of prey. They have long, sharp claws called talons, and they attack feet-first. The bald eagle catches fish. It swoops down to the water, grabs a fish and carries it away.

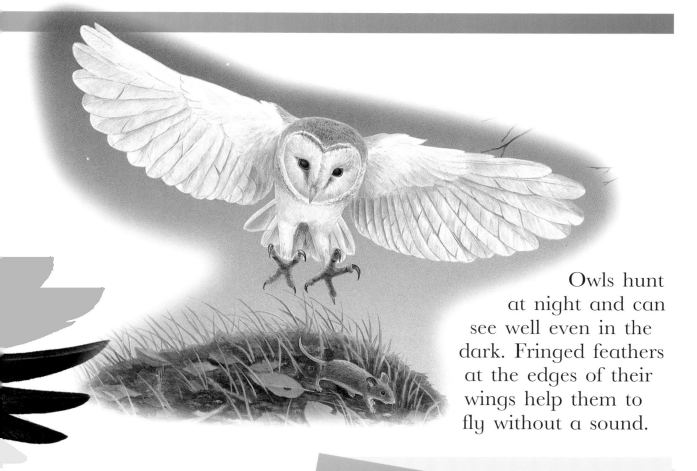

Owls hunt at night and can see well even in the dark. Fringed feathers at the edges of their wings help them to fly without a sound.

Groups of vultures gather at a kill. Vultures are scavengers. They usually eat animals that are already dead.

BEAKY BIRD CARD

Fold some card in half and cut a slit in the middle. Fold back the corners and push them inside out. Glue the card to more card,

leaving the beak free. Draw a bird's face round the beak. Now open and close the card.

Water birds

Many birds live near water. Some of them are good at swimming and some just wade at the water's edge. Seabirds feed on fish from the sea. Other birds nest close to rivers or lakes, where there is also plenty of food.

Ducks, geese, swans and most seabirds have webbed feet. These help them to swim quickly.

Puffins dive into the sea to catch fish. Their colourful beaks are so big that they can hold several small fish at a time. Huge groups of puffins make their nests on steep cliffs.

The heron has long legs like stilts
and a sharp beak like a dagger.
It stands very still at the
edge of a river or lake,
waiting for fish.
When the heron
spots one, it stabs
it with its beak
and gulps
it down.

The Arctic tern
travels further than
any other bird. It nests
near the North Pole,
then flies to the South
Pole at the other end
of the world for the
winter. In the spring,
it flies all the way back
to the North Pole again.

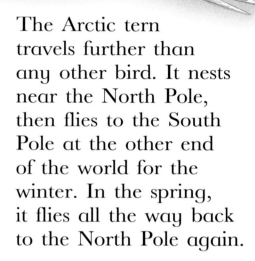

Penguins fish in the
icy cold seas near
the South Pole. They
have short wings like
flippers and swim so
fast that they look
as if they are flying
through the water.

Nests and eggs

All birds lay eggs that hatch into chicks. Most birds make soft nests in which to lay their eggs. They build them in safe places, away from enemies. Then the birds sit on their eggs to keep them warm until they hatch.

When a chick is ready to hatch, it uses a special tooth to chip a hole in its eggshell. When the hole is big enough, the chick pushes its way out, head first.

Crows build big, untidy nests high in treetops. The nests are made of sticks bound together with mud and moss. Inside, they are lined with a thick layer of soft wool or hair.

The chicks squawk for food.

The Indian tailor bird makes its nest by sewing leaves together with silk from a spider's web.

Swallows build cup-shaped mud nests high up on walls, out of reach of enemies.

The chicks are covered in fluffy down.

The plover does not make a nest. Instead, it lays its eggs on shingle, where the speckled eggs are well camouflaged.

Mammals

Mammals are animals whose bodies are covered with fur or hair. They feed their babies on milk. There are many different mammals. Most of them live on land, but some of them live in the sea.

Like many mammals, pigs give birth to several babies at a time. The piglets push and shove to take turns at drinking their mother's milk.

White-sided dolphin

Dolphins and whales are mammals that live in the sea. They cannot breathe underwater, so they come up to the surface to breathe.

Bats are the only mammals that can fly. They come out to hunt for food at night and roost during the day. Bats have furry bodies and leathery wings that stretch along their arm and finger bones.

A rabbit has a thick furry coat, like many mammals. Its fur keeps it warm and dry and protects it from injury. A rabbit can see, hear and smell very well. These sharp senses help it to look out for enemies.

Hunting

Many mammals are meat-eaters. This means that they have to catch other animals to eat. Animal hunters are armed with sharp teeth and claws, and can usually run very fast. Some animals hunt alone. Others work together to track down their prey.

Wolves and other wild dogs hunt in groups called packs. Each pack has a strong dog as a leader. The wolves work as a team to catch large animals.

The cheetah can run faster than any other animal. It silently slinks as close as it can to its prey, then sprints forwards and takes it by surprise.

Bears kill other animals with a swipe of their massive paws. The brown bear likes fish. It hooks salmon out of the water as they swim upstream to lay their eggs.

Living in a herd

Animals that eat plants spend most of their time grazing on grass or munching leaves. Many of them live on grasslands where there is nowhere to hide from hunters. Here it is safer for them to live together in large herds.

Wild horses move from place to place in herds. Each herd is made up of female horses and their foals. They are led by a stallion, a male horse.

Mother elephants and their babies live together in family groups, led by an older female. All the adults help to look after the babies.

Wildebeest live in enormous herds. Each herd travels great distances, looking for fresh grass to eat.

MAKE AN ELEPHANT CHAIN

Fold a long piece of paper into wide pleats. Draw an elephant on the top fold, with its trunk and tail touching each side, as shown. Cut out the elephant and open the paper out to make an elephant chain.

Marsupials

Marsupials are mammals with a pouch where their babies grow. The babies are tiny when they are born. They crawl up into their mother's pouch and live there until they are bigger.

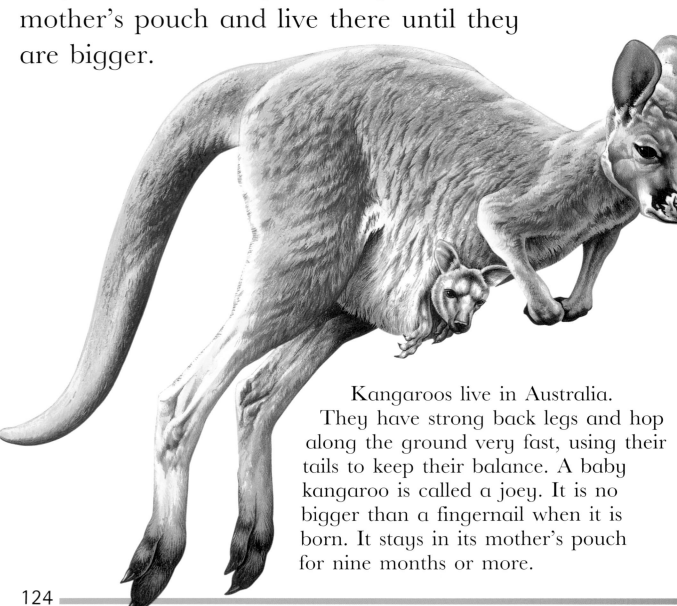

Kangaroos live in Australia. They have strong back legs and hop along the ground very fast, using their tails to keep their balance. A baby kangaroo is called a joey. It is no bigger than a fingernail when it is born. It stays in its mother's pouch for nine months or more.

Koalas are not bears. They are related to opossums. Koalas live in eucalyptus trees in Australia. Eucalyptus leaves are the only thing they eat. The leaves are so juicy that koalas never need to drink.

ROO PENCIL POUCH

Draw a big kangaroo outline on felt and cut it out. Cut out two ears and a pouch. Glue the ears to the roo and sew on the pouch. Draw a face and arms. Glue on beads for eyes.

Opossums live in trees. Baby opossums live for 10 weeks in their mother's pouch, then they climb out and cling tightly to her fur.

Water mammals

Some mammals spend most of their time in water. All water mammals are very good swimmers. Many of them dive deep underwater to catch fish. They can stay there for a long time, but they must return to the surface to breathe.

Otters live by rivers and seas. They have thick waterproof fur to keep them warm when they swim in cold water.

Hippotamuses live in Africa. During the day they wallow in rivers and lakes to keep cool. At night they go ashore to find grass and plants to eat.

The blue whale is the biggest animal in the world. It eats tiny shrimps called krill. It sieves them out of the water through a bony fringe in its mouth called a baleen.

Seals live in cold seas. They have a thick layer of fat called blubber to help keep them warm. Seals have flippers instead of back legs. They are fast swimmers and chase after fish, squid and octopus.

Strange mammals

From the tiniest mouse to the biggest whale, mammals come in every shape and size and some of them are very strange indeed.

The armadillo curls up when it is in danger. Its body is protected by bony plates of armour.

The aardvark lives on African grasslands. It eats insects called termites. When it finds a termite mound, it rips it open with its sharp claws and licks up the insects with its long, sticky tongue.

INVENT AN ANIMAL

Fold a long piece of paper into sections, as shown below. With a friend, take it in turns to draw part of a different animal on each section. When you open the paper out, you will see the animal you have invented!

The giraffe has long legs and a very long neck. It can stretch right up into the trees, to pull off juicy leaves and shoots that other animals cannot reach.

The platypus is furry. But it also has a flat beak and webbed feet, like a duck. It is one of the only mammals that lay eggs.

Animals in danger

Sadly, some animals are in danger of dying out forever. Thousands of animals die every year because their homes are destroyed when forests are chopped down. Other animals are killed by hunters.

Great auks are extinct now. 'Extinct' means that an animal has died out. Great auks were hunted for food until there were none left.

Tigers were in danger of dying out in India a few years ago, so a campaign was launched to save them. Special wildlife parks were set up where tigers could live safely.

130

The giant panda is one of the rarest animals in the world. There are fewer than 1,600 of them left. Pandas live in lonely parts of China. They only eat bamboo. Every few years the bamboo dies off. Some pandas die because they cannot find enough food.

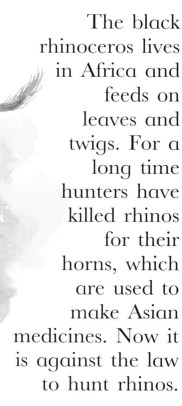

The black rhinoceros lives in Africa and feeds on leaves and twigs. For a long time hunters have killed rhinos for their horns, which are used to make Asian medicines. Now it is against the law to hunt rhinos.

Your Body

Inside you

Inside your body there are soft parts called organs that are hard at work all the time. Each organ has a special job to do to keep your body working properly. They all work together like the different parts of a machine.

Your brain, lungs, heart, liver, stomach and intestines are organs. They receive all the things they need from your blood, as it flows around your body.

Brain

Lungs

Heart

Liver

Stomach

Intestines

Your heart pumps your blood around every part of your body. It beats about 70 times a minute all the time you are alive.

Lay two fingers gently on the inside of your other wrist, below the creases. Count how many beats you feel in 15 seconds. Multiply this by four to find out how often your heart beats in a minute.

Your heart is about the same size as your clenched fist. As you grow, your heart grows bigger and stronger too.

135

Bones and joints

There are more than 200 bones that join together to make up your skeleton. This strong framework supports and protects the soft parts of your body. Without it, you would not be able to stand up or move about.

Skull

Ribcage

Spine

Pelvis

Bones are different shapes and sizes, depending on the job they do. Your skull forms a strong, bony case around your delicate brain. Your ribcage surrounds your chest to protect the organs inside.

The place where two bones meet is called a joint. The ends of the bones fit together or slide over each other smoothly.

Netball

Your joints allow you to perform many different activities.

Football

HALLOWEEN SKELETON

Draw a body, arms and legs like these on black card and cut them out. Make small holes with a pencil point where shown. Attach the arms and legs to the body with paper fasteners. Paint a skeleton on the body, using white paint. Hang the skeleton from a piece of thread to give your friends a fright!

Bicycling

Ballet

Tennis

Baseball

These children are bending and stretching their bodies in all sorts of sports.

137

Skin and hair

Your body is snugly wrapped up in your skin. Skin is a stretchy, waterproof covering that fits you like a glove. It protects your insides from dirt and germs, and helps to keep your body at the right temperature.

The skin on your fingertips has tiny ridges on it. These help you to grip things. Everyone has a different pattern of ridges.

Skin is not always the same colour. A brown colouring called melanin helps to protect skin from sunlight. Brown skin contains more melanin than white skin. People from hot, sunny places often have dark skin.

You are always growing new skin, because skin wears away. Hairs grow from the lower layer of your skin. Nerve endings help you to feel things. Sweat glands release sweat through tiny holes called pores. This cools you down.

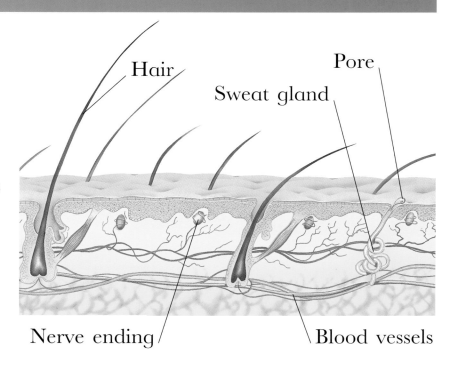

Hair

Sweat gland

Pore

Nerve ending

Blood vessels

When you are cold, you look pale because the blood vessels in your skin narrow to stop you losing more heat. Your hairs stand on end to trap body heat, and you shiver to warm up.

DETECTIVE WORK

To take a friend's fingerprints, roll each finger lightly on a stamp pad, then press it firmly on a piece of paper. Examine the prints with a magnifying glass to see the pattern on them.

The brain

Your brain is the control centre of your whole body. It keeps all the different parts working, and it never shuts down. Every time you move, your brain sends a message to part of your body, telling it what to do. You also use your brain to think and feel.

Your nerves are like a system of wires that run from your brain all around your body. They carry millions of messages between your brain and the rest of your body.

Nerves carry messages at very high speeds, so that you can react quickly to whatever is happening around you.

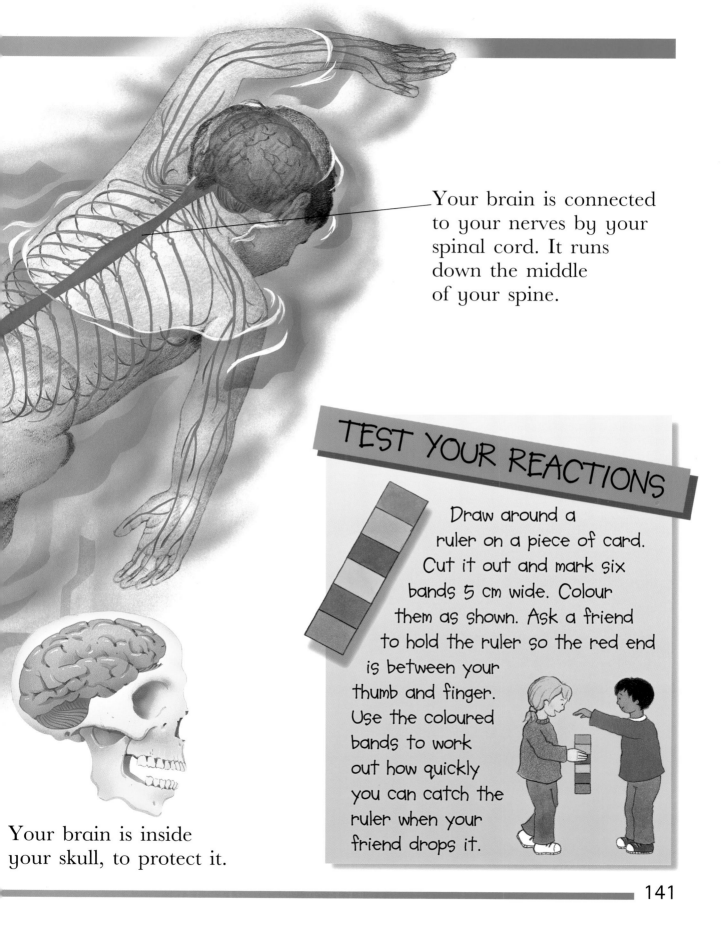

Your brain is connected to your nerves by your spinal cord. It runs down the middle of your spine.

Your brain is inside your skull, to protect it.

TEST YOUR REACTIONS

Draw around a ruler on a piece of card. Cut it out and mark six bands 5 cm wide. Colour them as shown. Ask a friend to hold the ruler so the red end is between your thumb and finger. Use the coloured bands to work out how quickly you can catch the ruler when your friend drops it.

Muscles

You have more than 600 muscles that help you to move every part of your body. Every time you jump, chew or just blink, you use different muscles. The brain controls all the muscles in your body, even when you are asleep.

Tendon

This muscle tightens to bend your arm.

This muscle tightens to straighten your arm.

Muscles are joined to bones by cords of tissue, called tendons. Muscles tighten to move bones. They only pull, so they usually work in pairs.

This gymnast is using hundreds of different muscles. She exercises to make her muscles stronger so she can bend, stretch and jump more easily.

FUNNY FACE TRICKS

Some of the tiny muscles in your face are very hard to use. Have a competition with your friends to see who can waggle their ears, flare their nostrils or arch their eyebrows – without moving any other part of their face at the same time.

Muscles in your face are hard at work all the time. Tiny muscles in your eyelids tighten to make you blink and wash your eyes with tear fluid. You do this about 20,000 times a day!

Breathing

You breathe all the time, even when you are asleep. The air that you breathe into your lungs contains a gas called oxygen, which you need to stay alive. Your lungs take oxygen from the air, then your blood carries it all the way around your body.

Windpipe

Lungs

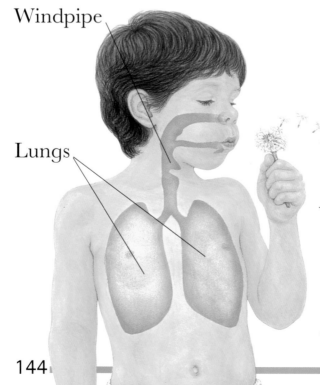

Your lungs are like big sponges. When you breathe in, they fill with air. When you breathe out or blow, they push out a waste gas called carbon dioxide that your body doesn't need.

144

People cannot breathe
underwater or in space
because there is no air.
Divers wear air tanks
on their backs. They
breathe in and out
through tubes that are
connected to the tank.

If there is something
blocking or tickling
your nose, you sneeze to
blow out all the dust and
germs. When you cough,
your body is getting rid
of any dust or germs that
have entered your lungs.

145

The senses

You use your eyes, ears, nose, skin and tongue to find out all about the world around you. You look around and you listen, smell, touch and taste things. You are using your five senses.

You feel things with your skin. The skin on fingertips is very sensitive. People who cannot see, 'read' special raised text, called braille, with their fingertips.

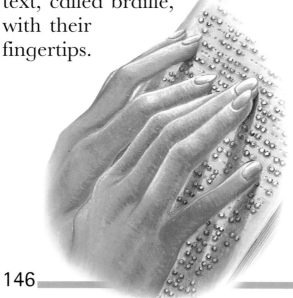

Think how hard it is to walk when you are blindfolded. Your eyes give you a lot of useful information. Your ears are able to pick up a huge range of sounds.

You taste things with your tongue, but your nose helps as well. It is hard to taste something properly unless you can smell it too.

Smells float about in the air and are picked up by your nose when you breathe in. You can tell the difference between thousands of different smells. Some things smell nice and others smell very nasty.

147

Eating

The food you eat should give you all you need to live and grow. You need to eat many different kinds of food to stay strong and healthy, because they contain the different things that are important for your body.

Fresh fruits and vegetables are packed with many things your body needs. It is important to eat many different types.

Your body takes all the energy you need to work and play from your food. This is why you need to eat regular meals throughout the day.

KEEP A FOOD DIARY

Draw a chart like this on a big piece of paper. Then write down what you eat at each meal every day for a week. How many different types of food do you eat?

Monday			
Tuesday			
Wednesday			
Thursday			
Friday			
Saturday			
Sunday			

Gullet

After you swallow food, it travels down your gullet to your stomach. It is mixed up into a mushy soup, then it moves along your intestine. All the useful bits of food filter through the wall of your intestines into your blood.

Stomach

Small intestine

Large intestine

Babies

You started life no bigger than a dot in your mother's tummy. You lived there for nine months, slowly growing until you looked like the baby shown here. Then, on your birth day, you were born and came out into a new world.

Womb

Womb opening

A baby grows in its mother's womb. It floats in a bag of warm, watery liquid to protect it. As her baby grows, the mother's womb stretches and her tummy gets bigger.

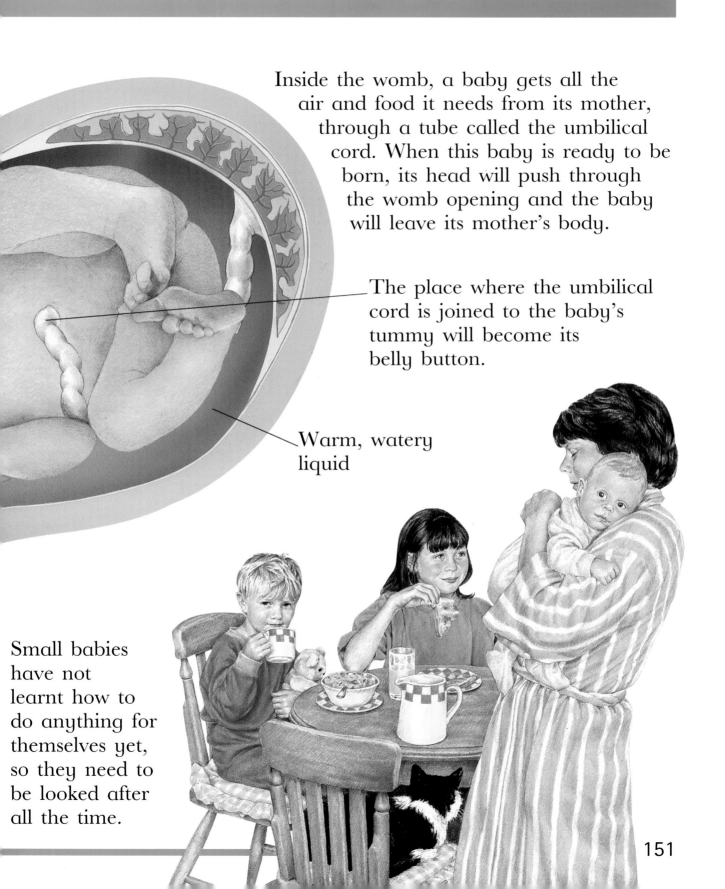

Inside the womb, a baby gets all the air and food it needs from its mother, through a tube called the umbilical cord. When this baby is ready to be born, its head will push through the womb opening and the baby will leave its mother's body.

The place where the umbilical cord is joined to the baby's tummy will become its belly button.

Warm, watery liquid

Small babies have not learnt how to do anything for themselves yet, so they need to be looked after all the time.

People
and Places

Houses and homes

Around the world, people live in all kinds of different homes. They build them out of materials they find nearby. Some houses are made of bricks or stone. Others are made of wood, mud or reeds.

Some people are nomads. This means that they move from place to place. These nomads in Mongolia live in round tents called 'yurts'.

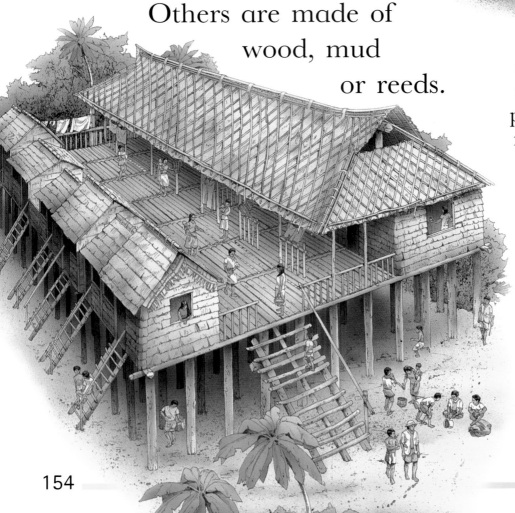

People who live near rivers and marshes often build their houses on stilts, like this house in Indonesia. It is raised high above the ground, safe from flooding.

In North Africa, some houses are built of mud, with thick walls and small windows to keep out the sun.

Tower blocks, like this one in Africa, are built in cities, where there is not much room for building. They contain many small homes called flats.

MAKE A STILT HOUSE

Cut and fold back the ends of four cardboard tubes, as shown. Tape them to the bottom of a cardboard box. Fold a piece of cardboard in half and tape it to the box to make a roof. Paint doors and windows on the box. Glue yellow drinking straws to the roof.

This house in the United States was built from bricks and wood. Both materials were easy to buy nearby.

155

Industry

Industries produce things that people need. Many industries make things, such as cars or buildings. Others produce the raw materials needed to make things, such as metals or oil.

The car industry produces cars. Billions of cars are made in factories every year. Most of them are put together on conveyor belts by robots.

Oil is needed to run machinery. There is oil buried under the sea, so oil rigs are built on high platforms in the sea. They drill deep into the seabed and pump the oil up to the surface.

Robot arm

Anchors hold oil platform in place

Helicopter landing pad

Crane

Drill

Many people work together to put up buildings. They use giant machines, like this crane, to lift massive pieces of buildings into place.

Scientists study chemicals. They work out how to make medicines, plastics and many other things that people use every day.

Religions

Many people around the world follow a religion. They believe in a god, or gods, who created the world and controls what happens in it. There are many religions. Each one has its own beliefs and traditions.

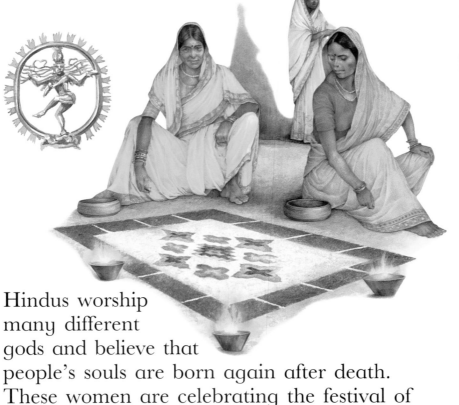

Hindus worship many different gods and believe that people's souls are born again after death. These women are celebrating the festival of light, Diwali. The god Shiva is shown, top left.

The religion of Jewish people is called Judaism. Jews believe in one god. They light candles in a special candlestick called a menorah during the festival of Hanukkah.

158

Muslims follow a religion called Islam, that was founded by the prophet Muhammad. They believe in a god called Allah, whom they worship in mosques. Their sacred book is called the Koran.

Minaret (tower) of a mosque

Church tower

Christians worship one god and believe that Jesus Christ was his son. Their holy book is the Bible. They worship in churches, chapels and cathedrals.

Buddists follow the teachings of the Buddha, seen here, and worship in temples. They believe that people are born again after death and that good deeds are rewarded in the next life.

Festivals

Festivals are large celebrations with music, dancing, colourful costumes and entertainments. Most festivals mark special days or events. Many are linked to a religion, while others may just celebrate the changing seasons.

Chinese people celebrate their New Year with a festival. Huge, brightly coloured dragons lead processions through the streets. People carry lanterns and let off fireworks.

In Sweden, people decorate a maypole and dance around it to celebrate Midsummer's Eve.

During a Japanese festival called Hinamatsuri, people float paper flowers or dolls down a river to make their problems go away.

DECORATE SOME EGGS

Ask an adult to make small holes in the ends of some eggs. Blow out the insides, and rinse and dry the eggs. To paper an egg, paste small squares of paper all over it. To paint an egg, paint patterns on one half first. Let the paint dry, then paint the other half.

At Halloween, people in the United States make spooky pumpkin lanterns to scare away evil spirits.

Many Christians celebrate Easter by giving each other decorated eggs, or eggs made from chocolate.

Transport

Tunnels and bridges

Tunnels and bridges make journeys shorter and easier. Bridges take roads and railways across obstacles, such as rivers and roads. Tunnels are cut through mountains and under rivers and seas.

To build tunnels, people cut through the rock with giant tunnelling machines, or blast huge holes using explosives.

Underground railways are built in tunnels that run deep under the ground beneath big cities. Here you can see that different lines, going in different directions, are built at different depths.

A crane lifts each section of the bridge into place.

Bridges are built of concrete, with steel beams and cables. First, the supports and ends of the bridge are firmly fixed to the ground or river bed. Then the part of the bridge that will carry the road or railway, called the deck, is lifted up on to the supports.

Section of the deck of the bridge

Pieces of the bridge are brought to the site by boat.

Submarines

Submarines can travel beneath the sea for many weeks without coming up to the surface. Many submarines are underwater warships that carry missiles and other dangerous weapons. Others are used to explore the depths of the sea.

1

2

The first submarine used in warfare could only carry one person. He had to turn the propeller, steer the submarine to an enemy ship and hook a bomb to its hull. This did not work, so the submarine was only used once.

Small underwater vessels are called submersibles. They dive deep under the sea to repair underwater cables and pipelines, or to carry out research. This one has robotic arms that can pick up and move things.

1 Propeller
2 Rudder
3 Hydroplane
4 Periscope

Large submarines have diesel or nuclear-powered engines that turn a propeller to move them through the water. The rudder steers and the hydroplane controls how deep a submarine goes. The captain uses a tube called a periscope to see what is above the surface of the water.

Travelling by air

Airliners are large aeroplanes with powerful jet engines. They can travel at speeds of more than 960 kilometres an hour. Airliners carry passengers great distances between countries very quickly.

This jumbo jet can carry more than 400 passengers. The pilot and co-pilot who fly the plane sit in the flight deck.

Fuel is stored inside the wings.

Seats where the passengers sit

Jet engine

Flight deck

The tail fin helps to keep the plane steady.

These flaps make the plane go up or down.

Flaps called ailerons make the plane turn left or right.

MAKE YOUR OWN GLIDER

For the wing, cut out a piece of stiff paper 24 cm by 13 cm. Tape the long sides together. Cut two slits in the taped edge and fold back two flaps. Cut out another piece of paper 20 cm by 3.5 cm for the tail. Fold the middle so it sticks up. Cut off 1 cm of the flat pieces each side of the tail, and then make flaps in the flat edges. Tape the wing and tail to a drinking straw, as shown, to make your plane. Attach paper clips to the front of the straw to make it heavier. Now try flying the plane.

When you have made your glider, try moving the flaps up and down, and the back of the tail from side to side. How does it affect the flight?

Rescue vehicles

When there is an accident or a fire, special vehicles rush to the scene. They are specially equipped to rescue people and save buildings. The police, the fire brigade and the ambulance service are the main emergency services.

The police use fast cars or bikes with sirens and flashing lights to reach the scene quickly.

Each emergency service does a different job. Ambulances rush injured people to hospital for treatment. They have beds and medical equipment inside them. Trained staff lift people into the ambulance on stretchers and look after them until they arrive at hospital.

170

Fire engines have extendable
ladders on turntables
that reach high
up buildings.

Firefighters point
their powerful hoses
at the flames to
put out the fire.

How Things Work

What is it made of?

The things around you are not all made out of the same material. They are made out of different materials depending on the job they have to do. Materials can be soft, hard, heavy, light, rough or smooth.

Do you know what your toys are made of? Soft things might be made of wool or fabric. Smooth things could be made of metal, plastic or glass.

Plastic

Fabric

Metal

Wool

Paper

Water

Ice

Steam

Everything is
either a liquid, a
solid or a gas. Liquids are
runny. Solids have a fixed
shape. Gases spread out to
fill the space they are in.
Some materials can change
from one thing to another.
Water is liquid, but when it
freezes it turns into solid ice.
If water boils, some of it
becomes a gas called steam.

Wood

Glass

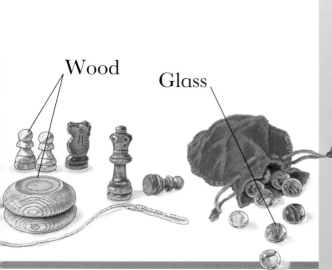

HOMEMADE ICE LOLLIES

Pour your favourite
fruit juice into some lolly
moulds and put them in
the freezer.

When the lollies have
frozen, hold them
upside down under
a warm tap for a
few seconds, then
gently slip them out
of the moulds.

Hot and cold

Heat never stays in one place. It moves around all the time, spreading out from warm places to colder ones. This is why hot things cool down and cold things warm up.

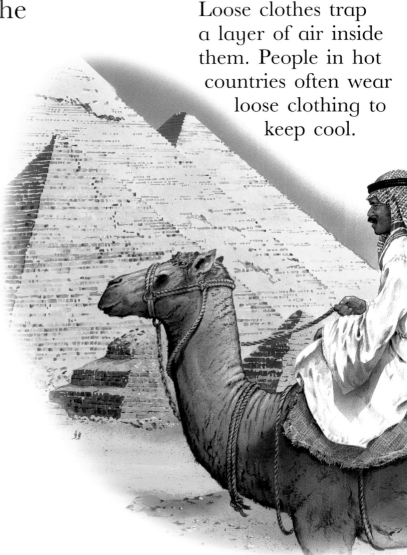

Loose clothes trap a layer of air inside them. People in hot countries often wear loose clothing to keep cool.

A radiator is filled with hot water. The heat spreads from the radiator to warm up the rest of the room.

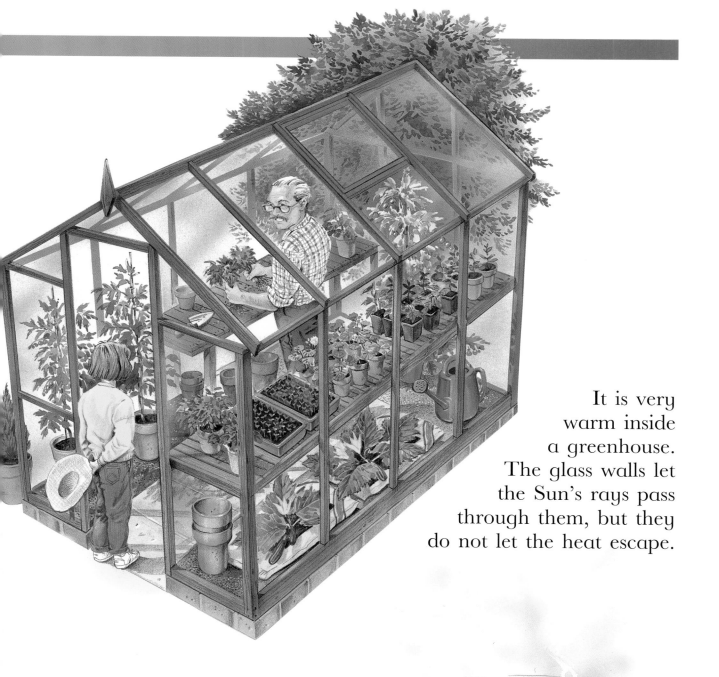

It is very warm inside a greenhouse. The glass walls let the Sun's rays pass through them, but they do not let the heat escape.

The water in this metal saucepan is being heated on a hotplate. The heat passes from the hotplate to the saucepan and then to the water. Metal is used to make saucepans because heat travels through it very easily.

Light

Without light, we would not be able to see. Most of our light comes from the Sun. It travels through space very fast. Light is made by hot or burning things. Fires, light bulbs and fireworks all make light.

The Moon cannot make its own light. The moonlight we see is really light from the Sun bouncing off the Moon. The Sun gives out light all the time, because it is a giant ball of burning gases.

MAKE SHADOW PUPPETS

Turn off the light in your room and ask a friend to shine a torch on to a wall beside you. Put your hands between the torch and the wall, then hold them in these different positions, to make animal shadows on the wall. Take it in turns to hold the torch and make animal shadows.

Dog

Giraffe

Bird

When light hits a smooth, shiny surface, like this puddle, it bounces back again and you see a reflection.

Light only travels in straight lines. It will not bend around things. If you block a Sun ray, you make a shadow. At midday, the Sun is high in the sky and your shadow is short.

Your shadow is always longer in the early morning or late afternoon.

Colours

Sunlight looks colourless, but in fact it is a mixture of different colours. You see all these colours in a rainbow, as the raindrops split the sunlight.

On a sunny day, you can make a rainbow with a hose. Stand with your back to the Sun and make a fine spray. You will see red, orange, yellow, green, blue, indigo and violet.

ROSE COLOUR SPECTACLES

Draw spectacle frames on a piece of thick card. Copy a pair of sunglasses you have at home to make them the right size. Cut the spectacles out and fold back the arms.

Tape coloured cellophane sweet wrappers across the eyeholes at the back of the frames. Colour and decorate the frames.

Blue, red and yellow are called primary colours. By mixing them together, you can make most other colours except white.

Many animals use colour to help them hide from other animals that might eat them. This leaf insect is the same colour as the leaves it sits on, so it is hard to spot.

The bright patterns on a butterfly's wings help it to attract a mate. The blue eye spots also trick hungry hunters into thinking it is not a butterfly.

Sounds

There are sounds around us all the time – voices, music, traffic. Every sound you hear is made by something vibrating. This means that it is moving backwards and forwards very quickly.

Sounds can also travel through solid things. This boy can hear the girl banging the saucepan through the tabletop.

Sounds move through the air in waves. When someone speaks to you, they make vibrations in the air. The sound waves travel through the air to you. Your ears pick up the vibrations and you hear sounds.

In a bottle organ, each bottle makes a different sound when you strike it. The more water there is in a bottle, the higher the sound it makes.

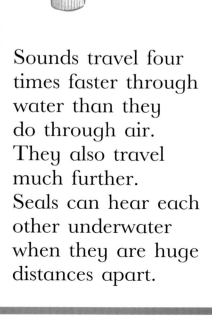

SEEING SOUNDS

You cannot see sound waves, but you can see their effects. Stretch some tin foil tightly over a bowl. Fasten it with an elastic band to make a drum. Put some grains of uncooked rice on the drum, then bang a tin tray next to it. The sound waves will make the rice jump about.

Sounds travel four times faster through water than they do through air. They also travel much further. Seals can hear each other underwater when they are huge distances apart.

183

Movement

Movement uses up energy, so all moving objects must get the energy that they need from somewhere. There are many different ways that they do this.

Inside a vehicle, there is an engine that burns fuel, such as diesel oil or petrol. When this fuel is burned, it releases energy that the vehicle uses to move.

Surfers use the sea's energy to move. They wait for a big wave, then surf along it as it breaks. They are carried forward by the movement of the water.

You get energy from the food you eat. When you ride a bike, you use up energy stored inside your body. You need to eat regularly so that you do not run out of energy.

Like all animals, these kangaroos get their energy from the food they eat.

You use your own energy to start a toboggan by giving it a push. When it is going downhill the toboggan has enough energy to keep moving by itself.

Magnets

Magnets can pull – or attract – things
towards them. Materials that are attracted
to magnets are called magnetic.
Most metals are magnetic,
but paper, plastic and
wood are not.

Non-magnetic
objects

Magnetic
objects

Collect objects from around your
home and test them with a magnet
to see which materials are magnetic.

North pole

South pole

North pole

South pole

The ends of a magnet are called its north and south poles. The two poles are different. The north pole of one magnet attracts the south pole of another magnet. Two north poles or two south poles push each other apart.

Scrapyards use giant magnets attached to cranes to lift scrap metal. The magnets are so strong that they can even lift up cars!

Electricity

Electricity can be used to make heat and light and to power all kinds of machinery. It runs through all the wires in your home. Small amounts can also be stored in batteries.

This toaster runs on electricity. You can plug machines into the sockets around your home to make them work. Take care when using electricity – you could get a dangerous electric shock.

Electricity will only flow along wires if there are no gaps in the circuit. When the lightbulb is connected to the battery like this, the light will switch on.

MAKE A SIMPLE CIRCUIT

Screw a small bulb into a bulb holder. Take two pieces of flex and strip 1 cm of plastic from the ends of each. Attach one end of each piece of flex to a screw of the bulb holder. Attach paper clips to the other ends and clip them to the battery terminals.

The lightning you see during a thunderstorm is electricity, but it is not the same as the electricity you use at home. Lightning is called static electricity.

Index

If you want to read about a subject, you can use this index to find out where it is in the book. It is in alphabetical order.

Acknowledgements

The publishers would like to thank the following artists for their contributions to this book:

Hemesh Alles, Marion Appleton, Mike Atkinson, Craig Austin, Julian Baker, Julie Banyard, John Barber, Andrew Beckett, Tim Beer, Richard Bonson, Derick Bown, Maggie Brand, Derek Brazell, Peter Bull, John Butler, Martin Camm, Jim Channel, Robin Carter, Adrian Chesterman, Dan Cole, Jeanne Colville, Tom Connell, Joanne Cowne, Peter Dennis, Sandra Doyle, Richard Draper, Brin Edwards, Colin Emberson, Diane Fawcett, James Field, Michael Fisher, Chris Fobey, Chris Forsey, Andrew French, Terence J. Gabbey, Peter Goodfellow, Ruby Green, Ray Grinaway, Terry Hadler, Nick Hawken, Tim Hayward, Karen Hiscock, David Holmes, Steve Holmes, Adam Hook, Christian Hook, Liza Horstman, Biz Hull, Mark Iley, Ian Jackson, Rob Jobson, Kevin Jones, Pete Kelly, Roger Kent, Tony Kenyon, David Kerney, Deborah Kindred, Steve Kirk, Mike Lacey, Stuart Lafford, Terence Lambert, Ruth Lindsay, Bernard Long, Chris Lyon, Kevin Maddison, Alan Male, Adam Marshall, Josephine Martin, David McAllister, Doreen McGuiness, Eva Melhuish, Steve Noon, Chris Orr, Nicki Palin, Darren Pattenden, Bruce Pearson, Liz Pepperell, Jane Pickering, Maurice Pledger, John Potter, Nigel Quigley, Sebastian Quigley, Elizabeth Rice, John Ridyard, John Rignall, Gordon Riley, Bernard Robinson, Eric Robinson, Eric Robson, Mike Roffe, David Russell, Mike Saunders, John Scory, Stephen Seymour, Rob Shone, Guy Smith, Clive Spong, Mark Stewart, Charlotte Stowell, Lucy Su, Treve Tamblin, Myke Taylor, Ian Thompson, Jean Paul Tibbles, Chris Turnball, Richard Ward, Ross Watton, Phil Weare, Rhian West James, Steve Weston, Lynne Willey, Ann Winterbotham, David Woods, Dan Wright, David Wright

Every effort has been made to credit the artists whose work appears in this book. The publishers apologise for any inadvertant omissions. We will be pleased to amend the acknowledgments in any future editions.